教育部、国家语委重大文化工程
　　"中华思想文化术语传播工程"成果
国家社会科学基金重大项目
　　"中国核心术语国际影响力研究"（21&ZD158）
"十四五"国家重点出版物出版规划项目
获评第二届向全国推荐中华优秀传统文化普及图书

典藏版 · 第一卷

Key Concepts in Chinese Thought and Culture

中华思想文化术语 2

《中华思想文化术语》编委会 编

外语教学与研究出版社
FOREIGN LANGUAGE TEACHING AND RESEARCH PRESS
北京 BEIJING

图书在版编目 (CIP) 数据

中华思想文化术语：典藏版. 第一卷. 2：汉英对照 /《中华思想文化术语》编委会编. -- 北京：外语教学与研究出版社，2023.12
ISBN 978-7-5213-4878-1

I. ①中… II. ①中… III. ①中华文化－术语－汉、英 IV. ①K203-61

中国国家版本馆 CIP 数据核字 (2023) 第 205209 号

出 版 人　王　芳
项目策划　刘旭璐
责任编辑　赵璞玉
责任校对　王海燕
封面设计　梧桐影
版式设计　孙莉明
出版发行　外语教学与研究出版社
社　　址　北京市西三环北路 19 号 (100089)
网　　址　https://www.fltrp.com
印　　刷　三河市北燕印装有限公司
开　　本　710×1000　1/16
印　　张　57
版　　次　2024 年 1 月第 1 版 2024 年 1 月第 1 次印刷
书　　号　ISBN 978-7-5213-4878-1
定　　价　349.00 元（全五册）

如有图书采购需求，图书内容或印刷装订等问题，侵权、盗版书籍等线索，请拨打以下电话或关注官方服务号：
客服电话：400 898 7008
官方服务号：微信搜索并关注公众号"外研社官方服务号"
外研社购书网址：https://fltrp.tmall.com

物料号：348780001

"中华思想文化术语传播工程"专家团队

(按音序)

Scholars Participating in the Project "Key Concepts in Chinese Thought and Culture: Communication Through Translation"

顾问 (Advisors)

李学勤 (Li Xueqin)　　　　　林戊荪 (Lin Wusun)
叶嘉莹 (Florence Chia-ying Yeh)　张岂之 (Zhang Qizhi)
楼宇烈 (Lou Yulie)　　　　　王　宁 (Wang Ning)

专家委员会 (Committee of Scholars)

主任 (Director)

韩　震 (Han Zhen)

委员 (Members)

晁福林 (Chao Fulin)　　　　陈德彰 (Chen Dezhang)
陈明明 (Chen Mingming)　　冯志伟 (Feng Zhiwei)
韩经太 (Han Jingtai)　　　　黄友义 (Huang Youyi)
金元浦 (Jin Yuanpu)　　　　静　炜 (Jing Wei)
李建中 (Li Jianzhong)　　　李雪涛 (Li Xuetao)
李照国 (Li Zhaoguo)　　　　聂长顺 (Nie Changshun)
潘公凯 (Pan Gongkai)　　　王　博 (Wang Bo)

王柯平（Wang Keping）	叶　朗（Ye Lang）
袁济喜（Yuan Jixi）	袁行霈（Yuan Xingpei）
张　晶（Zhang Jing）	张立文（Zhang Liwen）
张西平（Zhang Xiping）	郑述谱（Zheng Shupu）

特邀汉学家（Scholars of China Studies）

艾　恺（Guy Salvatore Alitto）	安乐哲（Roger T. Ames）
白罗米（Luminiţa Bălan）	包华石（Martin Joseph Powers）
陈瑞河（Madaras Réka）	狄伯杰（B. R. Deepak）
顾　彬（Wolfgang Kubin）	韩安德（Harry Anders Hansson）
韩　裴（Petko Todorov Hinov）	柯鸿冈（Paul Crook）
柯马凯（Michael Crook）	斯巴修（Iljaz Spahiu）
王健、李盈（Jan & Yvonne Walls）	魏查理（Charles Willemen）

学术委员会（Academic Committee）

白振奎（Bai Zhenkui）	蔡力坚（Cai Lijian）
曹轩梓（Cao Xuanzi）	陈海燕（Chen Haiyan）
陈少明（Chen Shaoming）	程景牧（Cheng Jingmu）
丁　浩（Ding Hao）	付志斌（Fu Zhibin）
干春松（Gan Chunsong）	郭晓东（Guo Xiaodong）
韩志华（Han Zhihua）	何　淼（He Miao）
何世剑（He Shijian）	胡　海（Hu Hai）
贾德忠（Jia Dezhong）	姜海龙（Jiang Hailong）
柯修文（Daniel Canaris）	黎　臻（Li Zhen）

李存山（Li Cunshan）	李恭忠（Li Gongzhong）
李景林（Li Jinglin）	林敏洁（Lin Minjie）
林少阳（Lin Shaoyang）	刘　佳（Liu Jia）
刘　璐（Liu Lu）	刘　青（Liu Qing）
吕玉华（Lü Yuhua）	梅缵月（Mei Zuanyue）
孟庆楠（Meng Qingnan）	裴德思（Thorsten Pattberg）
彭冬林（Peng Donglin）	乔　希（Joshua Mason）
任大援（Ren Dayuan）	邵亦鹏（Shao Yipeng）
沈卫星（Shen Weixing）	施晓菁（Lynette Shi）
陶黎庆（Tao Liqing）	童孝华（Tong Xiaohua）
王丽丽（Wang Lili）	王　琳（Wang Lin）
王明杰（Wang Mingjie）	王维东（Wang Weidong）
王　鑫（Wang Xin）	温海明（Wen Haiming）
吴根友（Wu Genyou）	吴礼敬（Wu Lijing）
夏　晶（Xia Jing）	谢远笋（Xie Yuansun）
辛红娟（Xin Hongjuan）	徐明强（Xu Mingqiang）
徐亚男（Xu Yanan）	许家星（Xu Jiaxing）
严学军（Yan Xuejun）	张　静（Zhang Jing）
张子尧（Zhang Ziyao）	章思英（Zhang Siying）
章伟文（Zhang Weiwen）	赵　桐（Zhao Tong）
赵　悠（Zhao You）	郑　开（Zheng Kai）
周云帆（Zhou Yunfan）	朱绩崧（Zhu Jisong）
朱良志（Zhu Liangzhi）	朱　渊（Zhu Yuan）
左　励（Zuo Li）	

前言

"中华思想文化术语"的定义可以表述为：由中华民族所创造或构建，凝聚、浓缩了中华哲学思想、人文精神、思维方式、价值观念，以词或短语形式固化的概念和文化核心词。它们是中华民族几千年来对自然与社会进行探索和理性思索的成果，积淀着中华民族的历史智慧，反映中华民族最深沉的精神追求以及理性思索的深度与广度；其所蕴含的人文思想、思维方式、价值观念已经作为一种"生命基因"深深融于中华子孙的血液，内化为中华民族共同的性格和信仰，并由此支撑起中华数千年的学术传统、思想文化和精神世界。它是当代中国人理解中国古代哲学思想、人文精神、思维方式、价值观念之变化乃至文学艺术、历史等各领域发展的核心关键，也是世界其他国家和民族了解当代中国、中华民族和海外华人之精神世界的钥匙。

当今世界已进入文化多元与话语多极时代。世界不同区域、不同国家、不同民族的文明，其流动融合之快、之广、之深超过历史任何时期。每个国家和民族都有自己独具的思想文化和话语体系，都应在世界文明、世界话语体系中占有一席之地，得到它应有的地位和尊重。而思想文化术语无疑是一个国家和民族话语体系中最核心、最本质的部分，是它的思想之"髓"、文化之"根"、精神之"魂"、学术之"核"。越来越多的有识之士认识到，中华思想文化蕴藏着解决当今人类所面临的许多难题的重要启示，中华民族所倡导的"厚德载物""道法自然""天人合一""和而不同""民惟邦本""经世致用"等思想,以及它所追求的"协和万邦""天下一家"、世界"大同",代表了当今世界文明的发展趋势,也因此成为国际社会的共识。越来越多的外国学者和友人对中华思想文化及其术语产生浓厚的兴趣,希望有更全面、更进一步的了解。

今天我们整理、诠释、翻译、传播中华思想文化术语,目的是立足于中华思想文化,通过全面系统的整理与诠释,深度挖掘其中既能反映中华哲学思想、人文精神、思维方式、价值观念、文化特征,又具跨越时空、超越国度之意义,以及富有永恒魅力与当代价值的含义和内容,并将其译成英语等语言,让世界更客观、更全面地认识中国,了解中华民族的过去和现在,了解当代中国人及海外华人的精神世界,从而推动国家间的平等对话及不同文明间的交流借鉴。

中华思想文化术语的整理、诠释和英语翻译得到了中国教育部、中国国际出版集团、中央编译局、北京大学、中国人民大学、武汉大学、北京外国语大学等单位的大力支持,得到了叶嘉莹、李学勤、张岂之、林戊荪、楼宇烈、王宁等海内外众多知名学者的支持。需要说明的是,"中华思想文化术语"这个概念是首次提出,其内涵和外延还有待学界更深入的研究;而且,如此大规模地整理、诠释、翻译中华思想文化术语,在中国也是首次,无成例可循。因此,我们的诠释与翻译一定还有待完善的地方,我们会及时吸纳广大读者的意见,不断提高术语诠释与翻译的质量。

2021 年 12 月 11 日

Foreword

By "key concepts in Chinese thought and culture" we mean concepts and keywords or phrases the Chinese people have created or come to use and that are fundamentally pertinent to Chinese philosophy, humanistic spirit, way of thinking, and values. They represent the Chinese people's exploration of and rational thinking about nature and society over thousands of years. These concepts and expressions reflect the Chinese people's wisdom, their profound spiritual pursuit, as well as the depth and width of their thinking. Their way of thinking, values, and philosophy embodied in these concepts have become a kind of "life gene" in Chinese culture, and have long crystallized into the common personality and beliefs of the Chinese nation. For the Chinese people today, they serve as a key to a better understanding of the evolutions of their ancient philosophy, humanistic spirit, way of thinking, and values as well as the development of Chinese literature, art, and history. For people in other countries, these concepts open the door to understanding the spiritual world of contemporary China and the Chinese people, including those living overseas.

In the era of cultural diversity and multipolar discourse today, cultures of different countries and civilizations of different peoples are integrating faster, in greater depth, and on a greater scope than ever before. All countries and peoples have their own systems of thought, culture, and discourse, which should all have their place in the civilization and discourse systems of the world. They all deserve due respect. The concepts in thought and culture of a country and its people are naturally the most essential part of their discourse. They constitute the marrow of a nation's thought, the root of its culture, the soul of its spirit, and the core of its scholarship. More and more people of vision have come to recognize the inspirations Chinese thought and culture might offer to help resolve many difficult problems faced by mankind. The Chinese hold that a man should "have ample virtue and carry all things," "Dao operates naturally," "heaven and man are united as one," a man of virtue seeks "harmony but not uniformity," "people are the foundation of the state," and "study of ancient classics should meet present needs." The Chinese ideals such as "coexistence of all in harmony," "all the people under heaven are one family," and a world of "universal harmony" are drawing increasing attention among the international community. More and more international scholars and friends have become interested in learning and better understanding Chinese thought and culture in general, and the relevant concepts in particular.

In selecting, explaining, translating, and sharing concepts in Chinese thought and culture, we have adopted a comprehensive and systematic approach. Most of them not only reflect the characteristics of Chinese philosophy, humanistic spirit, way of thinking, values, and culture, but also have significance and/or implications that transcend time and national boundaries, and that still fascinate present-day readers and offer them food for thought. It is hoped that the translation of these concepts into English and other languages will help people in other countries to gain a more objective and more rounded understanding of China, of its people, of its past and present, and of the spiritual world of contemporary Chinese. Such understanding should be conducive to promoting equal dialogue between China and other countries and exchanges between different civilizations.

The selection, explanation, and translation of these concepts have been made possible thanks to the support of the Ministry of Education, China International Publishing Group, the Central Compilation and Translation Bureau, Peking University, Renmin University of China, Wuhan University, and Beijing Foreign Studies University, as well as the support of renowned scholars in China and abroad, including Florence Chia-ying Yeh, Li Xueqin, Zhang Qizhi, Lin Wusun, Lou Yulie, and Wang Ning.

The idea of compiling key concepts in Chinese thought and culture represents an innovation and the project calls much research and effort both in connotation and denotation. Furthermore, an endeavor like this has not been previously attempted on such a large scale. Lack of precedents means there must remain much room for improvement. Therefore, we welcome comments from all readers in the hope of better fulfilling this task.

December 11, 2021

目录
Contents

1. āntǔ-zhòngqiān 安土重迁
   Attached to the Land and Unwilling to Move 1

2. bāguà 八卦
   Eight Trigrams 2

3. běnsè 本色
   Bense (Original Character) 3

4. bǐdé 比德
   Virtue Comparison 6

5. biàntǐ 辨体
   Style Differentiation 7

6. biécái-biéqù 别材别趣
   Distinct Subject and Artistic Taste 9

7. biéjí 别集
   Individual Collection 11

8. chéng 城
   Fortress / City 13

9. chǔcí,《Chǔcí》楚辞
   Chuci (Ode of Chu) 14

10. chúnwáng-chǐhán 唇亡齿寒
    Once the Lips Are Gone, the Teeth Will Feel Cold. 16

11. cídá 辞达
    Expressiveness 17

12 dàofǎzìrán 道法自然
Dao Operates Naturally. 18

13 dū 都
Capital / Metropolis 19

14 dúhuà 独化
Self-driven Development 21

15 fǎbù'ēguì 法不阿贵
The Law Does Not Favor the Rich and Powerful. 22

16 fēigōng 非攻
Denouncing Unjust Wars 23

17 gànchéng 干城
Shield and Fortress / Dukes and Princes 24

18 gāngróu 刚柔
Toughness and Softness 26

19 gémìng 革命
Changing the Mandate / Revolution 27

20 géwù-zhìzhī 格物致知
Study Things to Acquire Knowledge 28

21 guàyáo 卦爻
Trigrams / Hexagrams and Component Lines 30

22 guójiā 国家
Family-state / Country 31

23	guótǐ 国体	
	Guoti	33
24	guòyóubùjí 过犹不及	
	Going Too Far Is as Bad as Falling Short.	34
25	hǎinèi 海内	
	Within the Four Seas / Within the Country	35
26	hǎiwài 海外	
	Outside the Four Seas / Overseas	36
27	hé'érbùtóng 和而不同	
	Harmony but Not Uniformity	37
28	hòudé-zàiwù 厚德载物	
	Have Ample Virtue and Carry All Things	38
29	huà gāngē wéi yùbó 化干戈为玉帛	
	Beat Swords into Plowshares / Turn War into Peace	40
30	huàgōng / huàgōng 化工 / 画工	
	Magically Natural, Overly Crafted	41
31	huàdào 画道	
	Dao of Painting	43
32	huàlóng-diǎnjīng 画龙点睛	
	Add Pupils to the Eyes of a Painted Dragon / Render the Final Touch	44

13

33 huìxīn 会心
Heart-to-heart Communication 46

34 hùndùn 浑沌
Chaos 47

35 huófǎ 活法
Literary Flexibility 49

36 jiān'ài 兼爱
Universal Love 51

37 jiěyī-pánbó 解衣盘礴
Sitting with Clothes Unbuttoned and Legs Stretching Out 52

38 jīng（jīngshī）京（京师）
Capital of a Country 54

39 jīngjì 经济
Govern and Help the People / Economy 55

40 jīngshì-zhìyòng 经世致用
Study of Ancient Classics Should Meet Present Needs 57

41 jìngjiè 境界
Jingjie (Visionary World) 59

42 jìngshēngxiàngwài 境生象外
Aesthetic Conception Transcends Concrete Objects Described. ... 61

43 jū'ān-sīwēi 居安思危
Be on Alert Against Potential Danger When Living in Peace 63

44	jūn 君	
	Lord / Nobility / Monarch	64
45	jūnzǐ 君子	
	Junzi (Man of Virtue)	65
46	kāiwù-chéngwù 开物成务	
	Understand Things and Succeed in One's Endeavors	67
47	kūn 坤	
	Kun (The Earth Symbol)	68
48	lǐ 礼	
	Li (Rites / Social Norms / Propriety)	69
49	miàowù 妙悟	
	Subtle Insight	70
50	mínbāo-wùyǔ 民胞物与	
	All People Are My Brothers and Sisters, and All Things Are My Companions.	73
51	míngshí 名实	
	Name and Substance	74
52	mìng 命	
	Mandate / Destiny	75
53	qìxiàng 气象	
	Prevailing Features	76

15

54 qián 乾
   Qian 78

55 qǔjìng 取境
   Qujing (Conceptualize an Aesthetic Feeling) 79

56 réndào 人道
   Way of Man 81

57 rénwén 人文
   Renwen (Human Culture)..82

58 sānxuán 三玄
   Three Metaphysical Classics...84

59 shàngdì 上帝
   Supreme Ruler / Ruler of Heaven 85

60 shàngshàn-ruòshuǐ 上善若水
   Great Virtue Is Like Water..86

61 shényǔwùyóu 神与物游
   Interaction Between the Mind and the Subject Matter 87

62 shényùn 神韵
   Elegant Subtlety..89

63 shīchū-yǒumíng 师出有名
   Fighting a War with a Moral Justification 91

64 shīshǐ 诗史
   Historical Poetry..93

65　shī zhōng yǒu huà, huà zhōng yǒu shī 诗中有画，画中有诗
　　Painting in Poetry, Poetry in Painting..................95

66　shíshì-qiúshì 实事求是
　　Seek Truth from Facts..................97

67　sī 思
　　Reflecting / Thinking..................98

68　sīwén 斯文
　　Be Cultured and Refined..................99

69　sìduān 四端
　　Four Initiators..................100

70　sìhǎi 四海
　　Four Seas..................101

71　sìshū 四书
　　Four Books..................102

72　tǐ 体
　　Ti..................104

73　tiānrén-héyī 天人合一
　　Heaven and Man Are United as One...................106

74　tiānrénzhīfēn 天人之分
　　Distinction Between Man and Heaven..................107

75　tiānzǐ 天子
　　Son of Heaven..................109

17

76 wēnróu-dūnhòu 温柔敦厚
Mild, Gentle, Sincere, and Broad-minded 110

77 wénbǐ 文笔
Writing and Writing Technique 112

78 wénxué 文学
Literature / Scholars / Education Officials 114

79 wénzhāng 文章
Literary Writing 116

80 Wú-Yuè-tóngzhōu 吴越同舟
People of Wu and Yue Are in the Same Boat................................. 118

81 wǔjīng 五经
Five Classics.. 119

82 xiāoyáo 逍遥
Carefree... 121

83 xiǎorén 小人
Petty Man 122

84 xíng'érshàng 形而上
What Is Above Form / The Metaphysical 123

85 xíng'érxià 形而下
What Is Under Form / The Physical 124

86 xìngjì 兴寄
Xingji (Association and Inner Sustenance) 125

87 xìngqù 兴趣
   Xingqu (Charm) 126

88 xūyī'érjìng 虚壹而静
   Open-mindedness, Concentration, and Tranquility 128

89 xué 学
   Learn 129

90 yǎngmín 养民
   Nurture the People 131

91 yìshù 艺术
   Art 132

92 yìjìng 意境
   Aesthetic Conception 135

93 yìxìng 意兴
   Inspirational Appreciation 138

94 yǔzhòu 宇宙
   Universe / Cosmos 139

95 yuán 元
   Yuan (Origin) 140

96 zhèngzhì 政治
   Decree and Governance / Politics 142

97 zhīxíng 知行
   Knowledge and Application 143

19

98 zhǐgēwéiwǔ 止戈为武
Stopping War Is a True Craft of War. 145

99 zìqiáng-bùxī 自强不息
Strive Continuously to Strengthen Oneself 146

100 zǒngjí 总集
General Collection / Anthology 147

术语表 List of Concepts 150
中国历史年代简表 A Brief Chronology of Chinese History 155

āntǔ-zhòngqiān 安土重迁

Attached to the Land and Unwilling to Move

安于故土生活，不轻易迁往他处。这是传统农业社会一般民众普遍具有的一种思想观念和情感。其实质，首先是离不开土地，因为土地是农业社会人们赖以生产、生活的基本资源；其次是离不开祖宗坟茔和血亲家族，因为传统中国是宗法制社会，祖宗崇拜是基本信仰，聚族而居是社会常态。此外，离开自己生于斯长于斯的环境和社会，人们会感到不便或不安。这种思想观念和情感偏于消极或保守，但也体现了人们热爱家乡、热爱土地、热爱亲人、热爱和平的纯良品格。

Feeling attached to the native land and reluctant to move to another place. This was a widespread way of thinking and sentiment among the common people in a traditional agricultural society. In essence, it is because they depended on the land to make a living, since the land served as their basic resource for production and livelihood. Also, they were loath to leave the burial place of their ancestors as well as their family and relations. In the Chinese clan system, ancestor worship was a basic belief and living together with one's clan was the social norm. People felt it upsetting and inconvenient to leave the environment and society in which they grew up. This concept and sentiment may seem passive and conservative, but it reflects the Chinese people's simple love for their homeland, relatives, and a peaceful life.

引例 Citation：

◎安土重迁，黎民之性；骨肉相附，人情所愿也。(《汉书·元帝纪》)

（安于故土生活，不轻易迁往他处，是普通百姓共通的情性；亲人相互依存，不愿分离，是人们共有的心愿。）

Attached to the land and unwilling to move – this is the nature of the common people. Interdependent among relatives and reluctant to leave them – this is a shared feeling. (*The History of the Han Dynasty*)

bāguà 八卦

Eight Trigrams

由"—"（阳爻）和"--"（阴爻）每三个一组合成的一套符号系统。三"爻"合成一卦，共有八种组合，故称"八卦"。"八卦"的名称分别是乾（☰）、坤（☷）、震（☳）、巽（☴）、坎（☵）、离（☲）、艮（☶）、兑（☱）。古人认为"八卦"象征着自然或社会中的一些基本事物或现象，其基本的象征意义分别是天、地、雷、风、水、火、山、泽。古人借由"八卦"彼此之间的交互演变及其象征意义，来理解和阐发自然与社会的运行变化及其法则。

Each of the eight trigrams consists of three lines and each line is either divided (--) or undivided (—), representing yin or yang respectively. The eight trigrams are: *qian* (☰), *kun* (☷), *zhen* (☳), *xun* (☴), *kan* (☵), *li* (☲), *gen* (☶), and *dui* (☱). According to the ancient Chinese, the eight trigrams symbolized basic things and phenomena of nature or society and represented heaven, earth, thunder, wind, water, fire, mountain, and lake respectively. The ancient Chinese also used the interchanges and transformations of the eight trigrams and what they represented to understand and expound on natural and social changes and to explain why and how they took place.

引例 Citation：

◎古者包（páo）牺氏之王（wàng）天下也，仰则观象于天，俯则观法于地，观鸟兽之文与地之宜，近取诸身，远取诸物，于是始作八卦，以通神明之德，以类万物之情。(《周易·系辞下》)

（古时伏羲氏统治天下，仰头观察天上的物象，俯身观察大地的法则，观察鸟兽的斑纹以及地上适宜生养之物，近处取法于人体自身，远处取法于万物的形象，于是初始创作了"八卦"，以会通事物神妙显明的本质，以区分归类万物的情态。）

When Fuxi was the ruler under heaven, he looked up into the sky to observe celestial phenomena and looked down on the land to observe geographical features and examine the images of birds, animals, and all other things that existed on earth. He selected symbols from the human body close by and from various objects far away, and then invented the eight trigrams to explain the miraculous nature and distinguish the states of all things. (*The Book of Changes*)

běnsè 本色

Bense (Original Character)

原义指本来的颜色，引申指本来的样子、面貌。作为文学批评术语，主要有三种含义：其一，指符合文体规定的艺术特色和风貌；其二，指符合作家艺术个性的特色和风貌；其三，指作品中真率自然地贴近生活原貌、表达自己真实思想或感情的风格。本色不仅是对作者的要求，也是对作品的要求。

宋代文论中，本色多用于评述文体的特性；明清文论中，本色多指诗人作家的个性风格，也用来倡导不加雕饰地贴近生活原貌的创作风格。"本色"常与"当行"连用，相当于"本真"，往往与道家自然之道的思想相联系，用来反对过分雕琢的创作态度与作品风格。

The term originally referred to true colors and has been extended to mean true appearance. As a term of literary critique, *bense* (本色) has three meanings: 1) the artistic style and literary features that are compatible with a given genre; 2) the style and literary features that remain true to the writer's individual character; and 3) the style that makes it possible for the writing to remain true to the author's own experience and that gives truthful expression to his thoughts and feelings. *Bense* is not only a requirement for the writer but also for his works. In the literary criticism of the Song Dynasty, *bense* was often used to describe and evaluate the special qualities of different genres. In the literary criticism of the Ming and Qing dynasties, *bense* usually referred to the individual style of poets and writers and also those styles of writing that remained true to life experience and eschewed literary embellishment. *Bense* is often used together with *danghang* (当行 professionalism) to mean "original and genuine"; it is often associated with the Dao of nature in classical Daoist philosophy, in opposition to the attitude and styles that stress literary embellishment.

引例 Citations：

◎退之以文为诗，子瞻以诗为词，如教坊雷大使之舞，虽极天下之工，要非本色。（陈师道《后山诗话》）
（韩愈以写文章的方法来写诗，苏轼以写诗的方法来写词，就像教坊里的艺人雷大使跳女子舞蹈，虽然技巧高明无比，但并不符合诗词的本色。）

Poems written by Han Yu read like essays and *ci* lyrics by Su Shi read like poems. This is like Master Dancer Lei of the Song Palace Music School performing dances choreographed for women. Although they were good writers, what they wrote was incompatible with the original characters of the genres. (Chen Shidao: *Houshan's Understanding of Poetry*)

◎近来觉得诗文一事只是直写胸臆，如谚语诗所谓开口见喉咙者。使后人读之，如真见其面目，瑜瑕俱不容掩，所谓本色。此为上乘文字。(唐顺之《与洪方洲书》)

(最近觉得写诗作文只需要直接写出心中所想，就像俗语所说的"开口看见喉咙"。让后人读到这样的作品，就能看到作者的真面目，优点、缺点都不掩饰，这就是本色。能体现本色的作品才是最好的文字。)

Recently I have come to realize that in writing poetry or prose, all that is needed is to write what I have in mind. This is like the Chinese saying, "When you open the mouth, others can see your throat." When readers read such works, they will come to know what the author is actually like. Without hiding either strengths or weaknesses, the author makes his true character fully apparent. The writing that best embodies the author's original character is most desirable. (Tang Shunzhi: *Letter to Hong Fangzhou*)

◎世事莫不有本色，有相色。本色，犹俗言正身也；相色，替身也。(徐渭《〈西厢〉序》)

(世上之事莫不有本色，有相色。本色，好比说是本来之我；而相色，好比替身。)

Everything in the world has its true appearance and its surrogate. True appearance is what I am, while a surrogate is a substitute. (Xu Wei: Foreword to *Romance of the Western Chamber*)

bǐdé 比德

Virtue Comparison

用自然物包括动植物的某些特性比附人的道德品格。引申到文学审美领域，一般是用美好的事物直接比喻高尚的人格精神，将自然现象看作是人的某些精神品质的表现和象征，体现出儒家将审美与文艺道德化的思维模式。人比德于自然，意味着对自然的欣赏其实就是对人自身特别是人所具有的伦理品格的欣赏。后成为修辞与诗歌创作的一种方式。

The term means likening certain characteristics of things in nature, including plants and animals, to human virtues. When extended to the domain of literary appreciation, it generally involves likening desirable objects to a noble personality. To perceive a natural phenomenon as a reflection or symbol of human characteristics is typical of the Confucian school, which takes aesthetic quality as a moral standard for people as well as literature and arts. Likening humans to nature implies that appreciation of nature is actually appreciation of humanity itself, particularly its moral character. It later became a technique employed in rhetoric and poetry.

引例 Citations：

◎昔者君子比德于玉焉，温润而泽，仁也。(《礼记·聘义》)
（从前，君子的道德人格可以和美玉相比，温润而有光泽，体现出的就是仁。）

In the past, the moral integrity of a man of virtue was likened to fine jade, which is smooth, mellow, and lustrous, an exact embodiment of benevolence. (*The Book of Rites*)

◎及三闾《橘颂》，情采芬芳，比类寓意，乃覃及细物矣。(刘勰《文心雕龙·颂赞》)

(到了屈原创作《橘颂》，情感和文采都很出色，用橘来类比并寄托某些寓意，于是延伸到对细小事物的描绘了。)

By the time Qu Yuan wrote "Ode to the Orange," both his sentiment and literary style had become highly refined. He used orange to draw analogy and convey a certain message before preceding to describe details. (Liu Xie: *The Literary Mind and the Carving of Dragons*)

biàntǐ 辨体

Style Differentiation

辨明文学作品的体式与风格。指创作时根据所要表达的思想感情选择合适的文学体式与风格，从而创作出内容与形式高度和谐一致的优秀作品。古代的文学家在从事文学创作时往往首先考虑文章的体式。魏晋南北朝时的文学批评家们详尽探讨了各种文体的艺术特征和艺术规律，强调创作者应根据思想感情表达的需要选择相应的文体进行写作，并应严格遵守所选文体的创作风格、语言形式与表达技巧，这样才能写出优秀的作品。与之相对的是"破体"，指打破各类文章体式与风格的界限，使之相互融合。"辨体"有时也指辨别与追求高尚的文学品格与境界。

The term refers to the differentiation of the form and style of a literary work. It means that before putting words on paper, one needs to decide on the form and style appropriate to the thoughts and feelings to be expressed so as to produce a fine literary work with a high degree of harmony between form and content. In creating literary works, ancient scholars tended to decide on the style before writing. Literary critics in the Wei, Jin, and Southern and Northern dynasties discussed in detail the artistic features and rules of all literary styles and stressed that authors must choose an appropriate form or style to express their thoughts and sentiments and strictly follow the rules of the style, language form, and writing technique required by the chosen form or style. This, they believed, was the only way to create excellent literary works. Contrary to the term "style differentiation," the term *poti* (破体) or "breaking-down styles" refers to the integration of different styles or forms of literary works by breaking down their boundaries. Style differentiation sometimes refers to differentiating the form or style of a literary work in order to attain a lofty character and realm of literature.

引例 Citations：

◎夫情致异区，文变殊术，莫不因情立体，即体成势也。势者，乘利而为制也。（刘勰《文心雕龙·定势》）

（作品所表达的思想情趣既有所区分，文章的创作手法也要因之变化，但都是依照思想感情确定文章的体式，就着体式形成文章的气势。文章的这种气势，是就着文体自身的特点进行创作而形成的。）

Since literary works express different ideas, temperaments, and tastes, the writing skills and techniques used should also differ in order to suit the content. It is the content of a literary work that determines its style, which in turn gives strength to the work. Such strength comes from writing in accordance with the style of the literary work. (Liu Xie: *The Literary Mind and the Carving of Dragons*)

◎夫诗人之思，初发取境偏高，则一首举体便高；取境偏逸，则一首举体便逸。（释皎然《诗式·辩体有一十九字》）

(诗人刚开始构思的时候,如果取境偏于高迈,那么整首诗的意境就高迈;如果取境偏于飘逸,那么整首诗的意境就飘逸。)

When the poet starts to compose a poem, if his conception of the poem tends towards grandeur, then the aesthetic conception of the poem will be grand; if his conception of the poem is free and easy, so will the aesthetic conception of the poem be. (Shi Jiaoran: *Poetic Styles*)

◎先辨体裁,引绳切墨,而后敢放言也。(章太炎《国故论衡·文学总略》)
(先辨明文章体裁,遵循文章体式的要求分出段落,而后才敢放开写作。)

One should first decide on the style or form of an article, decide paragraphs following the rules required by the chosen style or form for the article, and then start writing. (Zhang Taiyan: *Overview of Traditional Chinese Scholarly Learning*)

biécái-biéqù 别材别趣

Distinct Subject and Artistic Taste

诗歌应具有的特殊题材和特殊的人生趣味。北宋以来,在黄庭坚(1045—1105)的倡导下,江西诗派追求学问,以议论入诗,忽略诗歌自身的感兴特点。南宋严羽(?—1264)对此深为不满,在《沧浪诗话》中提出这个概念,旨在划清诗与非诗的界限,说明诗歌的本质是吟咏情性,而不是堆砌书本知识、卖弄学问;诗歌重在表现感受、传达意味,而不是单纯阐发义理,诗的义理应融化在审美意象中。"别材别趣"的提出,说明文论家注意到了诗歌自身的审美特性,倡导回归唐诗的创作方式和风格。

Poetry should have its distinct subject and artistic taste. In the Northern Song Dynasty, inspired by Huang Tingjian (1045-1105), poets of the Jiangxi School used poetry as a means to express views on public issues. In doing so, they tended to overlook the use of inspiring and evocative language unique to poetic expression. In *Canglang's Criticism on Poetry*, literary critic Yan Yu (?-1264) of the Southern Song Dynasty expressed his dismay at this trend. He argued that poetry should have its distinctive subject and purpose and that poetry should express the poet's sentiment and emotion rather than piling book knowledge or showing off learning or presenting theories. The message of a poem should be expressed through its aesthetic imagery. The advocating of distinct subject and artistic taste by Yan Yu shows that by the time of the Southern Song Dynasty, literary critics had recognized the distinctive features of poetic expression and called for return to the creative style of poetry writing of the Tang Dynasty.

引例 Citations：

◎夫诗有别材，非关书也；诗有别趣，非关理也。（严羽《沧浪诗话·诗辨》）
（诗歌有特殊的题材，跟书本知识没有关系；诗歌有特别的旨趣，跟论理没有关系。）

Poetry has its distinct subject matter and is not about book learning. It also has distinct artistic taste and is not about presenting theories. (Yan Yu: *Canglang's Criticism on Poetry*)

◎三百年间虽人各有集，集各有诗，诗各自为体；或尚理致，或负材力，或逞辨博，少者千篇，多者万首，要皆经义策论之有韵者尔，非诗也。（刘克庄《竹溪诗序》）
（宋朝三百年之间，虽然人人有文集，集中都有诗，诗又各有自己擅长的体式，这些诗或者崇尚义理情致，或者自负才学，或者逞辩夸博，少的上千篇，多的上万首，全都是阐发儒家经义或论述时政对策的文章，只不过押上韵罢了，根本不能算诗。）

During the 300 years of the Song Dynasty, a lot of people published collections of literary works, many of which contained poems dealing with different subject matters. In these poems, some authors showcased their arguments, while others paraded their learning or indulged in scholarly debate. Some published 1,000 poems, and others published even 10,000 poems; but most of them were merely rhymed essays that expounded Confucian classics or discussed current policies. They were just not poetry. (Liu Kezhuang: Preface to *A Collection of Lin Xiyi's Poems*)

biéjí 别集

Individual Collection

汇集某一作家个人诗文作品的集子（与汇集多人诗文作品的"总集"相对）。西汉刘歆（？—23）《七略》有"诗赋略"，录有屈原（前340？—前278？）、唐勒、宋玉等66家的作品，皆以作家为单位，是图书"别集"之始。东汉以后别集渐繁，两汉魏晋南北朝别集见于《隋书·经籍志》的就有886部，历代文人学者几乎人人有集。只收诗作的称为诗集，单收文或诗文并收的称为文集。别集常以作家姓名、字号、谥号、籍贯、居住地等命名。别集保存了某一作家的全部传世作品，是作家心灵世界的真实展示，也是后人认识和研究作家思想与文学成就的主要材料。

The term refers to a collection of works by an individual author, in contrast to an anthology which amalgamates the works of many writers. In the Western Han Dynasty, Liu Xin (?-23) composed *Seven Categories*, one of the categories being "The Catalogue of *Shi* and *Fu*," which collects the literary works of 66 writers including Qu Yuan (340?-278? BC), Tang Le, and Song Yu. Organized by author, "The Catalogue of *Shi* and *Fu*" was regarded as the beginning of individual collections. Many more individual collections were compiled in the Eastern Han Dynasty, as exemplified by the 886 collections of writers from the Han through Wei and Jin to the Southern and Northern Dynasties, recorded in *The History of the Sui Dynasty*. Nearly every author had his own collection. Collections devoted to poetry were usually entitled collection of poems while those concerned with prose or both poetry and prose were entitled collection of writings. An individual collection might be entitled after the author's name, pen name, posthumous title, birth place, or residence. Containing all the major works of an author, an individual collection enables readers to learn about the author's aspirations and therefore provides a valuable source for the study of his ideas and literary achievements for later generations.

引例 Citation：

◎别集之名，盖汉东京之所创也。自灵均已降，属（zhǔ）文之士众矣，然其志尚不同，风流殊别。后之君子，欲观其体势而见其心灵，故别聚焉，名之为集。(《隋书·经籍志》)

（别集的名称，大概是东汉时创立。自屈原以下，写作文章的文士太多了，但他们各自的志向和崇尚不同，风格和遗韵也相差很大。后代的人想通过文章考察作家的风格气势并窥见其内心世界，于是把他们的作品单独汇总在一起，称之为"集"。）

What is known as *bieji* (别集) appeared in the Eastern Han Dynasty. Literary history since Qu Yuan witnessed an increasing number of creative writers with distinctive aspirations, preferences, literary features, and tastes. To examine the style, strength, as well as the spiritual world of a specific author, later generations put together all his works and called it *ji* (集) or collection. (*The History of the Sui Dynasty*)

chéng 城

Fortress / City

　　四周由城墙环绕的城邑。"城"本指城墙、城郭，是筑土而成的、具有军事防御及防洪功能的设施，城外一般挖有护城河。古代王朝国都、诸侯封地、卿及大夫的封邑，都以筑有城墙的聚落为中心，所以称为"城"。"城"音"盛（chéng）"，意思是"容纳民众"。其根本功能为保护民众，是"民惟邦本"这一政治理念的具体体现。

Cheng (城) is a city with walls surrounding it. The Chinese character for *cheng* originally referred to inner and outer city walls built of earth, with military defense and flood control functions. Usually, it was surrounded by a moat. In ancient times, the state capital of a monarch, the fief of a prince, and a manor estate granted by a monarch to a minister or a senior official all had a walled settlement as the center, hence the name *cheng*. The Chinese character for *cheng* is pronounced the same way as another character meaning accommodating. Here, *cheng* means having the capacity to accommodate people. The primary function of a *cheng* is to protect its residents. This is a concrete manifestation of the political notion that "people are the foundation of the state."

引例 Citations：

◎城者，所以自守也。（《墨子·七患》）

（城是可以用来守卫自己的[设施]。）

A fortress / city is a facility used to defend the people inside. (*Mozi*)

◎城，以盛民也。（许慎《说文解字·土部》）

（城是用来容纳百姓的。）

A fortress / city is for accommodating people. (Xu Shen: *Explanation of Script and Elucidation of Characters*)

◎城为保民为之也。（《榖梁传·隐公七年》）

（城是为了保护人民而修建的。）

A fortress / city is built to protect people. (*Guliang's Commentary on The Spring and Autumn Annals*)

chǔcí,《Chǔcí》楚辞

Chuci (Ode of Chu)

  楚辞是由屈原（前340？—前278？）创作的一种诗体，后来又成为代表中国古代南方文化的第一部诗歌总集，楚辞运用楚地（今湖南、湖北一带）的文学体式、方言声韵，叙写楚地的山川人物、历史风情，具有浓厚的地域特色，因而得名。"楚辞"之名，西汉初期已有之，后刘向（前77？—前6）辑录成集，收战国时期楚国人屈原、宋玉以及汉代淮南小山、东方朔（前154—前93）、严忌、王褒、刘向等人作品共16篇，后来王逸作《楚辞章句》时增加了自己的一篇，共17篇。楚辞通过独特的文体与文化内涵，反映出南方楚国文化的特点，抒情色彩浓厚，想象丰富，保存了上古许多神话故事，彰显出不同于《诗经》传统的一种全新的文学精神与文学体式，成为与《诗经》并驾齐驱的文学形态，后世称这种文体为"楚辞体"或"骚体"，称研究《楚辞》的学问为"楚辞学"。

Chuci (楚辞) was a poetic genre first attributed to Qu Yuan (340?-278? BC). It later became the title for the first anthology of poetry depicting the culture in south China. *Chuci* was so named because it made use of Chu (now Hunan and Hubei provinces) dialect, accent, and local special genres to describe the unique landscape, history, and folklore of the State of Chu. The term *chuci* first appeared in the early Western Han Dynasty, and later Liu Xiang (77?-6 BC) compiled a literary collection including 16 pieces written by Qu Yuan, Song Yu, Huainan Xiaoshan (a group of authors of the Western Han Dynasty), Dongfang Shuo (154-93 BC), Yan Ji, Wang Bao, and Liu Xiang. When Wang Yi later compiled *Annotations on the Odes of Chu*, he added a work of his own to the collection, making it an anthology of 17 works. Through its distinctive genre and unique cultural elements, *chuci* reflected the special culture of the Chu region in southern China. As a genre, *chuci* is characterized by profound emotions, wild imagination, and rich allusions to the remote historical mythology from the dawn of Chinese history. It demonstrates an innovative and distinctive literary genre and spirit, standing with *The Book of Songs* as twin literary pinnacles. Later generations called this genre *Chuci* Style or *Sao* Style (Flowery Style), and its research *chuci* studies.

引例 Citations：

◎固知《楚辞》者，体宪于三代，而风杂于战国，乃雅颂之博徒，而词赋之英杰也。(刘勰《文心雕龙·辨骚》)

(可以肯定，《楚辞》取法于三代的圣贤之书，但也掺杂有战国的风气，比起《诗经》来，要逊色一些，但却是词赋中的精品。)

It can be ascertained that *Odes of Chu* borrowed literary elements from the classics of the past ages, but also blended some stylistic features from the Warring States Period. Though less outstanding than *The Book of Songs,* they were masterpieces in poetry. (Liu Xie: *The Literary Mind and the Carving of Dragons*)

◎盖屈宋诸骚，皆书楚语，作楚声，纪楚地，名楚物，故可谓之"楚辞"。（黄伯思《新校〈楚辞〉序》）

（大体上说，屈原、宋玉的诸多骚体之作，都是用楚地的方言，用楚地的音乐，描写楚国的地理，称说楚地的风物，因此可称作"楚辞"。）

Generally speaking, the literary works of Qu Yuan and Song Yu used Chu dialect and exploited Chu rhythm and tunes to depict the landscape and scenery in Chu, hence called *chuci*, or odes of Chu. (Huang Bosi: Preface to *Odes of Chu [Revised Edition]*)

chúnwáng-chǐhán 唇亡齿寒

Once the Lips Are Gone, the Teeth Will Feel Cold.

嘴唇没有了，牙齿就会感到寒冷。比喻相互间关系密切，相互依存，有共同的利害关系。据《左传·僖公五年》载，晋国向虞国借道，以便攻打虞国的邻国虢国。虞国的大夫宫之奇向国君进谏说：虢是虞的屏障，虢亡，虞必随之而亡，虞和虢是唇亡齿寒的关系。这实际反映华夏民族自古以来重视邻国关系和与邻友善、务实的地缘政治思想。

When two things are interdependent, the fall of one will endanger the other. According to the early chronicle *Zuo's Commentary on The Spring and Autumn Annals*, when the State of Jin wanted to march through the State of Yu in order to attack Yu's neighbor, the State of Guo. Gongzhiqi, a minister of Yu, remonstrated with his ruler, saying, "Guo provides a protective shield for Yu.

If Guo falls, Yu will soon follow. The relationship between Yu and Guo is like that between lips and teeth." This shows that since ancient times the Chinese nation has been keen to maintain friendly ties with neighboring countries. It represents pragmatic geopolitical thinking of maintaining amity with close neighbors.

引例 Citation：

◎且赵之于齐楚，扞蔽也，犹齿之有唇也，唇亡则齿寒。今日亡赵，明日患及齐楚。(《史记·田敬仲完世家》)

(而且赵国对于齐、楚两国来说，就是屏障，就像牙齿有嘴唇一样。嘴唇没有了，牙齿就会感觉寒冷。今天 [秦国] 灭了赵国，明天就会祸及齐国和楚国。)

To the states of Qi and Chu, the State of Zhao serves as a protective shield, just like the lips protecting the teeth. Once the lips are gone, the teeth will feel cold. If Zhao is defeated by the State of Qin today, the same fate will befall Qi and Chu tomorrow. (*Records of the Historian*)

cídá 辞达

Expressiveness

说话、写文章要能简明扼要地表达内心的意思。孔子（前551—前479）反对过度追求辞藻华丽，强调文辞只要能确切而简洁地传达出思想感情即可，并倡导"文质彬彬"的审美观念。这一术语后来经过刘勰(465？—520)、韩愈（768—824）、苏轼（1037—1101）等人不断继承与发展，形成了中国文学追求语言自然凝练、反对过分雕琢的美学旨趣与风格。

The term means to put forth one's thoughts in a clear and concise way when speaking and writing. Confucius (551-479 BC) opposed excessive efforts in pursuit of extravagant writing styles. He stressed that writings need only to express one's ideas and feelings clearly and precisely, and he advocated a concept of aesthetics that valued the combination of elegance and simplicity. This concept was successively inherited and developed by Liu Xie (465?-520), Han Yu (768-824), Su Shi (1037-1101), and others, resulting in a Chinese literary style that strives for natural and pithy expression as opposed to extravagant embellishment.

引例 Citations：

◎子曰："辞达而已矣。"(《论语·卫灵公》)

（孔子说："言辞能把意思表达清楚就行了。"）

Confucius said, "It's good enough if you express yourself clearly." (*The Analects*)

◎辞至于能达，则文不可胜用矣。（苏轼《答谢民师书》）

（文辞如果能够做到达意，那么文采的运用也就无穷无尽了。）

If one can write expressively, his potential to achieve literary grace is boundless. (Su Shi: A Letter of Reply to Xie Minshi)

dàofǎzìrán 道法自然

Dao Operates Naturally.

"道"效法、顺应万物的自然状态。这一命题出自《老子》。"自然"指事物自主、自在的状态。"道"创造、生养万物，但"道"不会对万物发号施令，而是效法、顺应万物之"自然"。"道"与万物的关系，在政治哲学中表现为统治者与百姓的关系。统治者应遵循"道"的要求，节制自己的权力，以无为的方式效法、顺应百姓的自然状态。

Dao operates in accordance with natural conditions of all things. This idea first appeared in the book *Laozi*, according to which "natural" means the natural state of things. Dao creates and nurtures everything, yet it does not command anything. In political philosophy, the relationship between Dao and natural things implies that between the ruler and the people. The rulers should follow the natural requirements of Dao, which places limits on their power, and govern by means of non-interference to allow the people and affairs to take their own natural course.

引例 Citation：

◎人法地，地法天，天法道，道法自然。(《老子·二十五章》)
(人效法地，地效法天，天效法道，道效法万物之自然。)

Man patterns himself on the operation of the earth; the earth patterns itself on the operation of heaven; heaven patterns itself on the operation of Dao; Dao patterns itself on what is natural. (*Laozi*)

dū 都

Capital / Metropolis

国都，国君处理政事及所居的城邑。"都"与"邑"的区别是：有宗庙（陈列祖先和前代君主牌位）的城叫做"都"；没有宗庙的叫做"邑"。

宗庙是大夫以上贵族统治者祭祀祖先的庙宇，是祖先崇拜的产物、宗法制度的体现，也是"都"的根本标志。周朝时，各诸侯国的政治中心都叫做"都"；秦汉以后，统指国都、帝王的治所。后规模大、人口多的城邑都可称为"都"。

The term refers to the city in which a state ruler resided and conducted government affairs. The difference between a *du* (都) and a *yi* (邑) was that the former had an ancestral temple to enshrine the memorial tablets of ancestors and previous rulers while the latter did not. An ancestral temple used to be a place where rulers, the nobility, and senior officials made offerings to their ancestors. Therefore, an ancestral temple was a product of ancestral worshipping and a symbol of the patriarchal clan system. It is the defining structure of a *du*. During the Zhou Dynasty, the political center of all ducal states was called *du*. From the Qin and Han dynasties onward, *du* referred to the place where the emperor lived. Later, all cities large in scale and population were called *du*.

引例 Citations：

◎凡邑，有宗庙先君之主曰都，无曰邑。(《左传·庄公二十八年》)
（所有城邑中，有宗庙和前代君主牌位的叫做"都"，没有的叫做"邑"。）

All cities with ancestral temples to house the memorial tablets of ancestors and previous rulers are called *du* while those without are called *yi*. (*Zuo's Commentary on The Spring and Autumn Annals*)

◎国，城曰都者，国君所居，人所都会也。(刘熙《释名·释州国》)
（一国的城邑称为"都"，是因为它是国君居住、人口聚集的地方。）

When a city is called *du*, it is where the ruler of the land resides and where there is a large population. (Liu Xi: *Explanation of Terms*)

dúhuà 独化

Self-driven Development

指天地万物不假外力，自己独立生成、变化。由郭象（？—312）在《庄子注》中提出。具体而言，"独化"包含三重含义：其一，天地万物的生成和变化都是自然而然的。其二，天地万物的生成和变化都是各自独立的。其三，天地万物的生成和变化都是突然发生的，是没有原因和目的的。"独化"观念否定了造物主的存在，同时也否定了一物构成另一物发生与存在的原因。但就世界整体而言，"独化"而成的万物又处于某种和谐的关系之中。

The term indicates that all things in heaven and on earth do not depend on external forces. Rather, they take shape and change by themselves independently. It was put forward by Guo Xiang (?-312) in his *Annotations on Zhuangzi*. Specifically, the term contains three meanings. Firstly, all things in heaven and on earth form and change naturally. Secondly, all things in heaven and on earth form and change independent of one another. Thirdly, all things in heaven and on earth form and change suddenly, without any reason or purpose. The concept of self-driven development denies the existence of a creator. At the same time, it also denies that one thing causes the occurrence and existence of another. However, according to this concept, all things in the universe, naturally formed, co-exist in harmony.

引例 Citation：

◎凡得之者，外不资于道，内不由于己，掘然自得而独化也。（郭象《庄子注》卷三）

(事物凡得其自性者，不依赖于外在的道，不依从于内在的诉求，没有原因地自我获得而独立生成变化。)

All that which comes into existence on its own neither depends on external laws nor does it depend internally on itself. Without any reason it came into being by itself and remains independent. (Guo Xiang: *Annotations on Zhuangzi*)

fǎbù'ēguì 法不阿贵

The Law Does Not Favor the Rich and Powerful.

法律对一切人平等，对权贵也绝不徇情偏袒。古代法家主张，治理国家应该不分贵贱亲疏，一切依据法律规定而予以奖惩。其主旨强调公正执法，法律面前，人人平等。这一主张为历代推崇，是"依法治国"思想的重要来源之一。

The law treats everybody equally, not favoring the rich and powerful. The Legalists in ancient China argued that there should be no distinction between noble and poor or close and distant people; punishment or reward should be meted out strictly in accordance with the law. They believed in fairness in enforcing the law and treating everyone as equal before the law. This belief has been championed through the ages and is a major source of the notion of rule of law.

引例 Citation：

◎法不阿贵，绳不挠曲。法之所加，智者弗能辞，勇者弗敢争。刑过不避大臣，赏善不遗匹夫。(《韩非子·有度》)

(法律不偏袒权贵，墨线不随弯就曲。法律所制裁的，即便是智者也不能推脱、勇者也不敢争辩。惩罚罪过不回避大臣，奖励善行不遗漏百姓。)

The law does not favor the rich and powerful, as the marking-line does not bend. What the law imposes, the wise cannot evade, nor can the brave defy. Punishment for wrongdoing does not spare senior officials, as rewards for good conduct do not bypass the common man. (*Hanfeizi*)

fēigōng 非攻

Denouncing Unjust Wars

反对、禁止不义的战争。"非攻"是墨家的基本主张之一。墨家认为，违反道义的攻伐战争有着严重危害。不仅被攻伐的国家遭到极大破坏，发动战争的国家也会因战争造成大量的人民伤亡及财产损失，因此应该禁止不义的战争。墨家也通过实际的行动反对并阻止国家间的相互攻伐，并研究了用以防御攻伐的战术、器具。

Opposition to unjust warfare is one of the basic concepts in the Mohist School of thought. It regards immoral and aggressive wars as acutely harmful to society. Not only does the country being attacked suffer great damage, the people of the country that starts the war also suffer serious casualties and property losses. Therefore, Mohists held that unjust wars should be prohibited. They took specific measures to prevent aggressive wars between nations, and conducted research into defensive tactics and armaments.

引例 Citation：

◎今欲为仁义，求为上士，尚欲中圣王之道，下欲中国家百姓之利，故当若非攻之为说，而将不可不察者此也。(《墨子·非攻下》)
(现在想要施行仁义，力求成为上等士人，上要符合圣王之道，下要有利于国家百姓的利益，那么对于非攻之说，就不可不审察了。)

If one wishes to be humane and just and become a gentleman with high moral standards, he must both observe the way of the sage kings, and advance the interests of the state and the people. In order to achieve these goals, the principle of prohibiting unjust wars cannot be disregarded. (*Mozi*)

gànchéng 干城

Shield and Fortress / Dukes and Princes

本指盾与城，后用来比喻诸侯，以及国家政权、理论主张等的捍卫者。"干"本义指盾，是古代的一种防御性武器，引申为捍御；"城"即城墙或城郭，是具有防御功能的建筑设施。用"干城"比喻诸侯，与"崇城"（比喻天子）相对。称天子为"崇城"，表明天子地位之崇高、优越；称诸侯为"干城"，表示诸侯的职责是拱卫天子，必须服从天子号令。后泛指忠实得力的保卫者——不仅指地位低的人保卫地位高的人，有时也指地位高的人保卫地位低的人。

The term originally referred to shield and fortress, but was later used to mean dukes and princes, and then defenders of a regime, theory or proposition. *Gan* (干shield), a defensive weapon in old days, is used to mean to defend, while *cheng* (城) means inner and outer city walls or a fortress, a structure for defensive purposes. Dukes and princes were likened to *gancheng* (干城), in contrast with *chongcheng* (崇城), which means supreme city, referring to the Son of Heaven and indicating his supreme position. It is meant that dukes and princes, likened to shield and fortress, had the responsibilities to defend the Son of Heaven. Hence, dukes and princes must obey orders from the Son of Heaven. As it has evolved over time, the term generally referred to loyal and efficient defenders. Interestingly, it came to mean that not only people of lower ranks defend their superiors, but also people of high positions defend their subordinates.

引例 Citations：

◎天子曰"崇城"，言崇高也；诸侯曰"干城"，言不敢自专，御于天子也。(《初学记》卷二十四引《白虎通义》)

(天子称"崇城"，意思是说天子居于崇高、尊贵的地位；诸侯称"干城"，意思是说诸侯不敢擅自行动，必须听命于天子。)

The Son of Heaven is referred to as *chongcheng*, indicating his supreme and noble status, while dukes and princes are referred to as *gancheng*, meaning that they must not act on their own but pledge their obedience to the Son of Heaven. (*Debates of the White Tiger Hall*)

◎赳赳武夫，公侯干城。(《诗经·周南·兔罝（jū）》)

(雄赳赳的武士，是诸侯的保卫者。)

The valiant warriors are defenders of dukes and princes. (*The Book of Songs*)

◎天下有道，则公侯能为民干城。(《左传·成公十二年》)

(如果国家政治清明，那么诸侯们就能成为百姓的保卫者。)

With good governance, dukes and princes become defenders and protectors of their people. (*Zuo's Commentary on The Spring and Autumn Annals*)

gāngróu 刚柔

Toughness and Softness

人和事物所具有的两种相反的属性或德性。主要有三种含义：其一，就自然物或器物而言，"刚"指坚硬，"柔"指柔软。其二，就个人的品格而言，"刚"指为人刚毅、坚强，"柔"指温柔、谦逊。其三，就为政、执法的风格而言，"刚"指严厉，"柔"指宽宥。"刚柔"被认为是"阴阳"的某种具体表现。"刚"与"柔"之间的对立与调和是促成事物运动变化的根本原因。在具体事物或行事中，二者应达到某种平衡，"刚"与"柔"过度都是不好的、危险的。

Two opposing properties or qualities that objects and human beings possess. The term has three different meanings. First, when describing natural or manmade objects, *gang* (刚) means hard and *rou* (柔) means soft. Second, when describing human qualities, *gang* means strong and determined, while *rou* means gentle and modest. Third, when describing a style of governance or law enforcement, *gang* means stern and *rou* means lenient. *Gang* and *rou* are one of the manifestations of yin and yang. Their mutual opposition and accommodation are the basic causes of change, and they must achieve a certain balance within any object or action. Too much of either is inappropriate and dangerous.

引例 Citations：

◎是以立天之道曰阴与阳，立地之道曰柔与刚，立人之道曰仁与义。(《周

易·说卦》)

(所以确立天的法则为阴与阳，确立地的法则为柔与刚，确立人世的法则为仁与义。)

The laws governing the ways of heaven are yin and yang, those governing the ways of the earth are *rou* and *gang*, and those governing the ways of human society are benevolence and righteousness. (*The Book of Changes*)

◎刚柔相推，变在其中矣。(《周易·系辞下》)

(刚与柔相互推移转换，变化就在其中了。)

Change occurs when *gang* and *rou* interact. (*The Book of Changes*)

gémìng 革命

Changing the Mandate / Revolution

变革王命。"革"，变革；"命"，初指天命，后来指王命，即帝王的政令或帝王的统治权。犹言江山易主、改朝换代，即推翻旧政权，建立新政权。古人认为，"王命"源于"天命"（上天的意志），故"革命"本质上是实施变革以应"天命"。而"革"是宇宙的基本规律，"革命"是这一规律的具体体现；判断"革命"合法性与成功的依据，则在于"革命"的领导者是否顺应了上天的意志和民众的意愿。近代以降，"革命"转指社会、政治、经济制度的重大变革。

The term means taking power from a ruler. *Ge* (革) means to change or remove. *Ming* (命) first referred to the mandate of heaven and later came to mean a ruler's decrees and his mandate to rule. Changing the mandate usually involves replacing a ruler and a change of dynasty, in other words, overthrowing an old regime and establishing a new one. People in ancient China believed that a ruler's mandate to rule was ordained by heaven and therefore any change of the mandate should in essence be carried out in response to the will of heaven. However, change is a basic law of the universe, and the removal of a ruler's mandate is a specific expression of this law. The legitimacy and success of such change depend on whether those who lead the change do so in response to the will of heaven and the popular desire of the people. In modern times, the term is used as an expression meaning revolution, denoting major social, political or economic changes.

引例 Citation：

◎天地革而四时成，汤武革命，顺乎天而应乎人。(《周易·彖下》)
（天地有阴阳的变化而形成一年四季。商汤、周武王变革天命[推翻旧政权，建立新政权]，是顺应了上天的旨意和人民的意愿。）

Changes of yin and yang in heaven and earth give rise to the four seasons. Following the mandate of heaven and complying with the wishes of the people, King Tang and King Wu overthrew old regimes and established the Shang and Zhou dynasties respectively. (*The Book of Changes*)

géwù-zhìzhī 格物致知

Study Things to Acquire Knowledge

在与事物的接触中体认人伦日用之道。"格物""致知"出自《礼记·大学》，与诚意、正心、修身、齐家、治国、平天下并称"八条目"。"致知"

在于"格物",二者密切相关,故有时并称"格致"。历代学者对"格物致知"的含义有多种不同的理解:或强调在对事物的接触中穷究其"理";或强调亲自实践以掌握各种德行、技艺;或以心意所在为"物",进而以内心的修正为"格物"。

The term means to understand how we should conduct ourselves through our contact with things. "Studying things to acquire knowledge" comes from *The Great Learning*, a section of *The Book of Rites*. Together with "being sincere in thought," "rectifying one's mind," "cultivating oneself," "regulating one's family well," "governing the state properly," and "bringing peace to all under heaven," they are collectively known as the "eight essential principles." Knowledge is acquired through the study of things. Since the two are closely related, they are sometimes together called "study and acquire." Throughout history scholars have had varied understandings of the meaning of the term. Some emphasize a thorough inquiry of principles in contact with things. Others stress personal practice in order to master all kinds of moral conduct and skills. Still others consider their intentions as things, thus reforming their innermost thoughts as studying things.

引例 Citations:

◎ 事皆有理,至其理,乃格物也。(《二程外书》卷二)
(事物皆有其理,穷究其理,就是"格物"。)

All things have their own principles. An exhaustive inquiry into the principles means the study of things. (*More Writings of the Cheng Brothers*)

◎ 格物如《孟子》"大人格君心"之"格"。(《传习录》卷上)
("格物"就如同《孟子》中所言"大人格正君主之心"之格正之义。)

Gewu (格物) means setting things right, just like what is said in *Mencius*: A great man may rectify a ruler's mind. (*Records of Great Learning*)

guàyáo 卦爻

Trigrams / Hexagrams and Component Lines

"卦"是由"—"和"--"排列组合而成的一套符号系统，其中的"—"为"阳爻"，"--"为"阴爻"。每三"爻"合成一卦，可得"八卦"。每六"爻"合成一卦，可得"六十四卦"。"卦爻"的产生与占筮有关。古人通过分取蓍草，演算其变化之数，从而确定卦爻，以预测吉凶。后人为卦爻赋予各种象征意义，并用以理解和阐发包括人事在内的天地万物的运行变化及其法则。

A gua (trigram / hexagram) is a system of symbols consisting of undivided lines (——) and divided lines (— —). The undivided line (——) is a yang line while the divided one (— —) a yin line. Three lines make a trigram, and there are eight such trigrams. When six lines are put together, they together make 64 hexagram combinations. Trigrams / hexagrams and component lines were created partly for the purpose of divination. Ancient Chinese people used yarrow stalks to make hexagrams, calculated the variations they suggested, and consulted them for the purpose of divination. Later on, people used trigrams / hexagrams and component lines symbolically to explain the changes and the laws regulating the changes that occurred in people and everything else, and why and how these changes took place.

引例 Citations：

◎八卦成列，象在其中矣；因而重之，爻在其中矣。(《周易·系辞下》)
（八卦创立分列，万物的象征就在其中了；根据八卦重成六十四卦，所有的爻就都在其中了。）

When the eight trigrams were invented, they embodied the images of all things. When the eight trigrams were multiplied by eight trigrams and permuted into the 64 hexagrams, all the 384 lines were included. (*The Book of Changes*)

◎圣人有以见天下之动，而观其会通，以行其典礼，系辞焉以断其吉凶，是故谓之爻。(《周易·系辞上》)
（圣人看到天下万物的运动变化，观察其中的会合贯通之处，从而施行制度礼仪，在"爻"下附系文辞以判断吉凶，所以称之为"爻"。）

When sages saw the changes or events happening under heaven, they observed the similarities of the events and responded with appropriate rites and rituals. They judged their implications of the changes by obtaining explanations from the *yao*. (*The Book of Changes*)

guójiā 国家

Family-state / Country

古代指诸侯和大夫的领地。古代诸侯的封地称"国"，大夫的封地称"家"。"国家"是"国"与"家"的合称。在古代中国，家庭、家族、国家都是依据血缘、宗法关系构建起来的，在组织结构上具有共通性。这就是所谓的"家国同构"。后演变指一国的全部疆域。近代以来，"国家"又指由一定疆域、人民和政权机构共同构成的政治实体。

Family-state referred to the land owned by feudal lords and officials in ancient China. The land of a feudal lord was called "state" and the land of an official was called "family." In ancient China, family, clan and country shared common structural features, all founded on the basis of blood relationships. This is the so-called "commensurability of family and state." Family-state later referred to the entire territory of a country. In modern times, the term is also used to denote a polity encompassing a territory, a people, and a government.

引例 Citations：

◎君子安而不忘危，存而不忘亡，治而不忘乱，是以身安而国家可保也。(《周易·系辞下》)

(君子安居时不忘危险，生存时不忘灭亡，天下太平时不忘记祸乱，如此自身就能安全、国家就能保全。)

A man of virtue and talent should be aware of potential danger in time of peace, keep in mind possible peril in time of security, and be vigilant of turmoil in time of order. Then he can keep himself safe and his country preserved. (*The Book of Changes*)

◎人有恒言，皆曰"天下国家"。天下之本在国，国之本在家。(《孟子·离娄上》)

(人们常说"天下国家"。"天下"的根本在于"国"，"国"的根本在于"家"。)

People often mention the following three together: all under heaven, the state, and the family. The root of all under heaven is in the state. The root of a state is in the family. (*Mencius*)

guótǐ 国体

Guoti

主要有三种不同的含义：其一，指辅佐国君的重要大臣。这是一种比喻的说法，即国家犹如人的身体，而辅佐国君的大臣犹如这个身体的重要组成部分。其二，指国家的法令制度。其三，指国家的体统或尊严。

The term, literally meaning the state and the body, has three meanings. First, it refers to the important ministers who help the sovereign ruler govern the state. Figuratively, the term suggests that the state is a human body and the ministers are the major components of the body. Second, it refers to the constitution and laws of a state. Third, it means national polity or dignity.

引例 Citations：

◎君之卿佐，是谓股肱，故曰国体。(《穀梁传·昭公十五年》范宁集解)
(辅佐国君的执政大臣，就像人的大腿和胳膊，所以称作"国体"。)

Ministers are like the arms and legs of the sovereign ruler. They constitute the major components of the country. (Fan Ning: *Annotations on Guliang's Commentary on The Spring and Autumn Annals*)

◎国体具存，纪纲不紊。(姚莹《与陆制军书》)
(国家的典章制度完备，政策法令的运行不紊乱。)

The national legal system is well enacted, and the laws and regulations are orderly implemented. (Yao Ying: *A Letter to General Lu*)

guòyóubùjí 过犹不及

Going Too Far Is as Bad as Falling Short.

事物超过一定的标准和没有达到标准同样是不好的。儒家以礼作为个人言语行事及其与天地万物关系的标准，并根据礼的要求判断言行的"过"或"不及"。孔子（前551—前479）分别用"过"与"不及"评价自己的两位学生，认为二者在未能达到礼的要求这一点上是一样的。如果能够按照礼的要求达到无过、无不及的中道，即具备了"中庸"的美德。

It is just as bad to go beyond a given standard as to fall short of it. Confucian scholars use rites as the standards both for individuals' words and actions, and for their relationship with everything in the world. They also judge people's words or actions against the requirements of the rites to see whether they have gone too far or fallen short. Confucius (551-479 BC) evaluated one of his students as "going too far" and another as "falling short," considering them to be the same in both failing the requirements set by the rites. If a person can follow the middle way by not going too far or falling short, then he has achieved the virtue of "the Golden Mean."

引例 Citation：

◎子贡问："师与商也孰贤？"子曰："师也过，商也不及。"曰："然则师愈与？"子曰："过犹不及。"(《论语·先进》)

（子贡问孔子："子张和子夏谁更好一些？"孔子说："子张行事过度，而子夏常有不及。"子贡问："那么子张这样更好一些吗？"孔子说："过与不及一样，都是不好的。"）

Zigong asked Confucius, "Which one is more virtuous, Zizhang or Zixia?" Confucius replied, "Zizhang tends to go too far, while Zixia often falls short." Zigong further asked, "In that case, is Zizhang better?" Confucius said, "Going too far is just as bad as falling short." (*The Analects*)

hǎinèi 海内

Within the Four Seas / Within the Country

"四海之内",即古代中国疆域以内。古人认为中国的疆域四周环海,各依方位称"东海""南海""西海"和"北海",合称"四海"。"海内"即指"四海"所环绕的疆土。它隐含着古人以海为界的国土意识,是农耕文明的反映。

Within the Four Seas means within the territory of China. The ancient Chinese thought China's territory was surrounded by the Four Seas (the East, West, North, and South seas). Within the Four Seas refers to the landmass surrounded by the Four Seas. It reflected the ancient Chinese belief that the seas were the natural boundary of a country, demonstrating the influence of an agriculture civilization.

引例 Citations:

◎今欲并天下,凌万乘,诎敌国,制海内,子元元,臣诸侯,非兵不可。(《战国策·秦策一》)

(如果想吞并天下,凌驾大国之上,使敌国屈服,控制海内,统治百姓,臣服诸侯,就非用武力不可。)

If our country wants to conquer all under heaven, rise above the big powers, subdue enemy states, control the territory within the Four Seas, govern the subjects and rule over the feudal lords, military force is indispensable. (*Strategies of the Warring States*)

◎海内存知己，天涯若比邻。（王勃《杜少府之任蜀州》）

（四海之内都会有知己，纵使远隔天涯海角也如近邻一样。）

If you have a bosom friend within the Four Seas, even at world's end he remains close to you. (Wang Bo: Seeing Off a Friend Who Has Been Appointed to a County Post in Shuzhou)

hǎiwài 海外

Outside the Four Seas / Overseas

"四海之外"，指古代中国疆域之外、国外，也指边远地区。古人认为中国疆域四周环海，各依方位称"东海""南海""西海"和"北海"，合称"四海"，所以称中国以外的地方为海外。其中隐含着古人以海为界的国土意识。它体现出古人以自我为中心而又具开放性的空间感，及其对于境外遥远地方的向往。

Outside the Four Seas refers to the territory outside China, foreign lands, or remote areas. The ancient Chinese thought that China's territory was surrounded by the Four Seas (the East, West, North, and South seas). Therefore, places outside China were outside the Four Seas. It reflected the ancient Chinese belief that the seas were the natural boundary of a country. It also suggested that the ancient Chinese were on the one hand self-focused and on the other open-minded, longing to explore the unknown world outside the Four Seas.

引例 Citation：

◎相（xiàng）土烈烈，海外有截。(《诗经·商颂·长发》)
（相土威武勇猛，边远地区的人都对他一齐顺服。）

Xiangtu was so brave that he was recognized and extolled even by those outside the Four Seas. (*The Book of Songs*)

hé'érbùtóng 和而不同

Harmony but Not Uniformity

在尊重事物差异性和多样性的基础上实现整体的和谐共存。"同"与"和"是对待、安顿社会群体的两种态度。"同"指对事物差异性的抹杀，"和"则意味着对事物差异性的保存与尊重。不同的事物彼此间相互辅助、补充，才能组成一个充满生机、富于创造性的和谐整体。

The term means achieving overall harmonious co-existence on the basis of respecting differences and diversity. Uniformity and harmony are two different attitudes to treating and accommodating social groups. Uniformity means obliterating differences in everything while harmony is to keep and respect the differences. Allowing different things to complement and supplement each other will create a harmonious whole full of vitality and creativity.

引例 Citations：

◎夫和实生物，同则不继。(《国语·郑语》)

（不同的事物相互调和而生成新的事物，只有相同的事物则难以有延续。）

Harmony begets new things; while uniformity does not lead to continuation. (*Discourses on Governance of the States*)

◎君子和而不同，小人同而不和。(《论语·子路》)

（君子与人和谐相处却不会盲目附和，小人盲目附和而不能真正和谐相处。）

A man of virtue pursues harmony but does not seek uniformity; a petty man seeks uniformity but does not pursue harmony. (*The Analects*)

hòudé-zàiwù 厚德载物

Have Ample Virtue and Carry All Things

　　以宽厚的德性承载天下万物。多指以宽厚之德包容万物或他人。古人认为，大地的形势和特质是宽厚和顺的，它承载万物，使万物各遂其生。君子取法于"地"，要像大地一样，以博大宽厚的道德容纳万物和他人，包含了对自身道德修养及人与自然、社会和谐一体的追求。这是中国人参照大地山川状貌和特质树立的治国理政和为人处事的理念和理想。它和"自强不息"一起构成了中华民族精神的基本品格。

This term means that one should be broad-minded and care for all things and people. Ancient Chinese believed that with its topography and other natural features being generous and peaceful, the earth sustained all things in the world, allowing them to grow and develop in keeping with their own nature.

Men of virtue model themselves on the earth, and just like the earth, care for all things and fellow human beings with open heart and virtue. This embodies the pursuit of moral cultivation and harmony among people and between people and nature. It represents the Chinese views and ideals on governance and human relationship, which were inspired by the formation and features of mountains and rivers in China. Together with the notion of constantly exerting oneself for self-improvement, it forms the fundamental character of the Chinese nation.

引例 Citations：

◎地势坤，君子以厚德载物。(《周易·象上》)

（大地的气势厚实和顺，君子应以宽厚美德容载天下万物。）

Just like the earth, which is generous and peaceful, a man of virtue should have ample virtue and accommodate all things. (*The Book of Changes*)

◎地势之顺，以地德之厚也。厚，故万物皆载焉。君子以之法地德之厚，而民物皆在所载矣。(陈梦雷《周易浅述》卷一)

（大地的形势是和顺的，因为大地具有宽厚的品德。因其宽厚，所以能承载万物。君子效法大地的宽厚品德，百姓、万物就都能被包容了。）

The peaceful nature of the earth is due to its virtue of generosity. Thus, it can accommodate and provide for all things. By modeling himself on the earth, a man of virtue should care for all people and all things. (Chen Menglei: *A Simple Account of The Book of Changes*)

huà gāngē wéi yùbó 化干戈为玉帛

Beat Swords into Plowshares / Turn War into Peace

消除仇怨，变战争为和平，变冲突为友好。"干""戈"是用于防御和进攻的两种武器，借指战争、武力冲突；"玉""帛"指圭、璋等玉器和束帛，是古代诸侯会盟、诸侯与天子朝聘时互赠的礼物，后来用于表示和平共处之意。它反映了华夏民族自古崇尚和平、愿意化解暴力冲突的美好期待。

The term means to eliminate animosity in order to turn war into peace and turn conflicts into amity. *Gan* (干) and *ge* (戈) are two weapons of war which were used for defense and attack respectively. *Yu* (玉) and *bo* (帛) mean jades (such as jade tablets and jade ornaments) which were gifts exchanged between feudal lords and tribute paid to monarchs. In time, *yu* and *bo* acquired the meaning of peace and co-existence. This term reflects the Chinese people's long-standing aspiration for peace and goodwill to dissolve conflict and violence.

引例 Citation：

◎上天降灾，使我两君匪以玉帛相见，而以兴戎。(《左传·僖公十五年》)
(上天降下灾祸，使我[秦、晋]两国国君没有带着玉帛会面，却发动了战争。)

Heaven has struck disaster, bringing our two sovereign lords (of the states of Qin and Jin) to face each other, not with jades and silks, but with the instruments of war. (*Zuo's Commentary on The Spring and Autumn Annals*)

huàgōng / huàgōng 化工 / 画工

Magically Natural, Overly Crafted

品评文学艺术作品风格自然与否的术语。"化工"指作品的工巧自然天成，毫无雕琢痕迹，达到了出神入化的地步；"画工"则是指作品的工巧由刻意雕琢而成，技巧虽高明，但缺乏自然韵味。"化工"是艺术家的作品，"画工"可以说是匠人的作品。这个评价标准，由明代李贽（1527—1602）《杂说》提出，与他所提倡的写文章要有真情、真心是一致的。从文化渊源上来说，"画工"与"化工"的区分，其实来自道家的纯任自然、弃绝机巧的思想。明代文士大都倡导文艺放任天然，否定雕琢模仿的创作立场。

The expressions are about the naturalness of literary and artistic works. The first one, "magically natural," means that a literary or artistic work is completed naturally and achieves the acme of perfection without any sign of craft. The second, "overly crafted," means that a work is meticulously crafted, but it is overly elaborate in style while lacking naturalness and spontaneity. "Magically natural" is used to refer to works accomplished by artists while "overly crafted" is used to describe works done by craftsmen. These two standards were proposed by Ming writer Li Zhi (1527-1602) in his "Random Thoughts," which echoed his idea that writings must reflect the author's true sentiments. Culturally, the distinction between "magically natural" and "overly crafted" is rooted in the Daoist thought of being harmonious with nature while forsaking excessive skills. Most Ming scholars favored literary naturalism and rejected elaboration and imitation.

引例 Citations:

◎吴生虽妙绝，犹以画工论。摩诘得之于象外，有如仙翮谢笼樊。吾观二子皆神俊，又于维也敛衽无间（jiàn）言。（苏轼《王维、吴道子画》）

（吴道子的技巧虽然绝妙，只能说是画工之作。王维的高妙之处则是超越了所描绘的物象，就像仙鸟离飞笼子。我看这两位技法都很高超，对于王维则更钦敬，没有任何可挑剔之处。）

Wu Daozi had superb technical skills, but his paintings were over crafted. What is remarkable about Wang Wei is that he gave free rein to his imagination in his paintings, like a bird that had broken free from its cage. Both of them were highly skilled, but I like Wang Wei better; I can find no fault in his works. (Su Shi: The Paintings of Wang Wei and Wu Daozi)

◎《拜月》《西厢》，化工也;《琵琶》，画工也。夫所谓画工者，以其能夺天地之化工，而其孰知天地之无工乎？（李贽《杂说》）

(《拜月亭》《西厢记》属于"化工"之作，《琵琶记》则是"画工"之作。之所以称"画工"，是人们认为它能够取代天地的造化之功，可是，谁知道天地本就没有这样的造化之工呢？）

The Moonlight Pavilion and Romance of the Western Chamber were works of magical naturalness, whereas A Tale of the Pipa was an overly crafted work. The latter shows that an attempt made to outdo the magic of nature has proved impossible to achieve. (Li Zhi: Random Thoughts)

huàdào 画道

Dao of Painting

绘画之道。有广狭二义：狭义指绘画的各种技法；广义则指画作中蕴含的文化理念、人格精神、艺术风格和审美追求，是"道"与"技"的完美融合。"道"决定画所要表现的思想主题、艺术法则和美学风格；画是"道"的具体表象，寄托了画家的文化理念、人格精神、艺术风格和审美追求。故道以画显，画因道而获得提升。杰出的画家追求技进乎道、艺与道合。画道，不仅包含了宇宙自然之道，而且折射了社会人生之道，彰显出中国固有的人文精神。

The term has both broad and narrow meanings. Interpreted narrowly, it means various painting techniques. Interpreted broadly, it means the cultural values, personality, artistic style, and aesthetic aspiration embodied in a painting, suggesting a perfect fusion of Dao and skills. Dao determines the theme a painting conveys as well as the painting's artistic principles and aesthetic style. A painting is a concrete image that illustrates Dao. It reflects the cultural principles followed by the painter as well as his personality, artistic style, and aesthetic aspiration. Therefore, paintings illuminate Dao, which in turn enhances the paintings. Prominent painters seek to access Dao through refining their skills and epitomizing Dao in artwork. The Dao of painting not only encompasses the Dao of nature, but also the Dao of social life, demonstrating the commitment to humanism inherent in the Chinese culture.

引例 Citations：

◎夫圣人以神法道，而贤者通；山水以形媚道，而仁者乐。不亦几乎？（宗

炳《画山水序》）

（圣人精神上效法道，而德才杰出的人可以通达于道；山水以其自然形质婉转契合道，使仁者对之喜爱。这难道不是很微妙吗？）

Sages follow Dao with their spirit. Men of virtue and talent may comprehend and practice Dao. Mountains and rivers conform to Dao through their natural shapes. That is why they are loved by benevolent people. Isn't this subtle and profound? (Zong Bing: On the Creation of Landscape Paintings)

◎画之道，所谓宇宙在乎手者，眼前无非生机。（董其昌《画禅室随笔·画源》）

（绘画之道，就是宇宙自然的神奇都能够通过手表现出来，呈现于眼前的全是有生命的景象。）

The Dao of painting enables one to use his hand to depict the wonder of nature and present to viewers a scene full of life. (Dong Qichang: *Essays from Huachan Studio*)

huàlóng-diǎnjīng 画龙点睛

Add Pupils to the Eyes of a Painted Dragon / Render the Final Touch

比喻文学艺术创作中在紧要处着墨或写出关键性的词句，以创造出最奇妙的神韵和意境来。孟子（前372？—前289）认为，观察一个人，最好观察他的眼睛，因为眼睛最容易表露一个人内心的善良和丑恶。东晋顾恺之（345？—409）画人物，曾数年不肯轻易下笔点睛。他强调人物传神之关键在于画出眼神。南朝画家张僧繇（yáo）绘画技术高超，传说他曾为画好的龙点上眼珠，龙即刻腾空而去。故后世用"画龙点睛"强调文学艺术创作中应抓住要诀，使形象更加生动传神。

The term is a metaphor about giving the finishing touch, which means providing critical details or key words in an artistic or literary work in order to lend it charm and aesthetic conception. Mencius (372?-289 BC) believed that when observing a person, one should look directly into his eyes because the eyes reveal his nature, be it good or evil. When painting portraits, Gu Kaizhi (345?-409) in the Eastern Jin Dynasty did not add pupils to the eyes in haste. He stressed that the key to painting a vivid portrait lied in painting the eyes. Zhang Sengyao, a painter of the Southern Dynasties, was well known for his excellent painting skills. Legend has it that his painted dragons flew into the sky as soon as he finished their pupils. The term is thus used by later generations to underline the importance of applying critical touches to add life and charm to a literary or artistic work.

引例 Citation：

◎ 又金陵安乐寺四白龙，不点眼睛，每云："点眼即飞去。"人以为妄诞，固请点之，须臾雷电破壁，两龙乘云腾去上天，二龙未点眼者见在。（张彦远《历代名画记》卷七）

（[张僧繇]在金陵安乐寺墙壁上画了四条白龙，他没有给龙点上眼睛，常说："点上眼睛，龙立刻就会腾空飞走。"人们都认为他的话荒唐虚妄，一再请他点上眼睛，[张僧繇只好提笔点睛，]即刻天空雷电交加，两条龙乘云腾空而去，而另两条没点眼睛的龙还留在墙壁上。）

Zhang Sengyao painted four white dragons on the wall of the Anle Temple in Jinling. But he did not paint pupils to their eyes, saying that once he did, the dragons would fly into the sky. People considered his words absurd and repeatedly urged him to add pupils to the dragons' eyes. He eventually did it on two of the four dragons. Suddenly, lightning and thunders struck, and the two dragons with pupils added to their eyes flew into the clouds. The other two remained on the wall. (Zhang Yanyuan: *Famous Paintings Through History*)

huìxīn 会心

Heart-to-heart Communication

不需言说而彼此心领神会。一般是指志趣、性情投合的朋友心意相通，能够互相理解和欣赏。特指自然美欣赏和文艺作品审美中主客体交融的境界。作者创作出美的意境，而欣赏者心领神会，感受到心与物高度融合及心心相印带来的快乐与慰藉。

The term refers to a situation in which people understand each other without the need to utter a single word. It generally means the spontaneous understanding reached by close friends who share common interests, aspirations, and dispositions. In particular, it refers to an aesthetic state in which the subject and the object interact with each other smoothly with no barrier between them, or in which an artist creates a marvelous image and a viewer appreciates it with emotion and understanding. The culmination of such an experience is joy and satisfaction derived from the perfect harmony between the human heart and its surroundings.

引例 Citations：

◎简文入华林园，顾谓左右曰："会心处不必在远，翳然林水，便自有濠濮间想也，觉鸟兽禽鱼自来亲人。"（刘义庆《世说新语・言语》）

（梁简文帝到华林园游玩，转过头对左右随从说："合人心意的地方不一定遥远，这里林木蔽空，其间一湾流水，便自然会产生庄子游于濠水桥上、垂钓于濮水的遐想，觉得鸟兽和鱼儿都主动和人亲近。")

When Emperor Jianwen of Liang in the Southern Dynasties was touring the Hualin Garden, he turned to his followers and said, "A place which prompts heart-to-heart communication need not be far. This garden is shadowed by trees and has a stream meandering through. Such a place makes one think of Zhuangzi strolling on the bridge of the Haoshui River and angling in the Pushui River, where birds and fish seemed eager to get close to him." (Liu Yiqing: *A New Account of Tales of the World*)

◎《三百篇》美刺箴怨皆无迹，当以心会心。(姜夔《白石道人诗说》)
(《诗经》中的颂美、怨刺与劝谏都没有明显的痕迹，欣赏时应当以心会心。)

The Book of Songs contains odes, satires, and admonitions, but all are veiled. One must engage in a heart-to-heart communication to appreciate them. (Jiang Kui: *The Poetry Theory of Baishi Daoren*)

hùndùn 浑沌

Chaos

"浑沌"又作"混沌"，有两种不同含义：其一，指天地分化形成以前宇宙浑然一体的状态。常以未分化之"气"言之。天地万物皆由"浑沌"分化演变而成。其二，特指《庄子》一则寓言中的中央之帝。中央之帝浑沌无七窍，被南海之帝儵（shū）和北海之帝忽凿开七窍而亡。庄子（前369？—前286）以此形象寓指人无知无识、无善恶彼我之分，与整个世界浑然一体的状态。

The term has two meanings. First, it refers to the state of one whole mass that existed before the universe took shape, often said to exist before *qi* (vital force) emerged. The multitude of organisms on earth all emanated from this state. Second, it refers to Chaos, king of the Central Region in a fable in *Zhuangzi*. According to the fable, Chaos had no eyes, nose, mouth or ears. Shu, king of the South Sea, and Hu, king of the North Sea, drilled seven apertures into Chaos and killed him. Zhuangzi (369?-286 BC) used this story to show the state of chaos of the world in which there is neither knowledge or wisdom, nor distinction between good and evil.

引例 Citations：

◎说《易》者曰："元气未分，浑沌为一。"（王充《论衡·谈天》）
（论说《周易》的人言道："元气没有分化之时，浑然一体。"）

Those who commented on *The Book of Changes* said, "Before *qi* (vital force) appeared, the world was in a state of formless chaos."（Wang Chong: *A Comparative Study of Different Schools of Learning*）

◎南海之帝为儵，北海之帝为忽，中央之帝为浑沌。儵与忽时相与遇于浑沌之地，浑沌待之甚善。儵与忽谋报浑沌之德，曰：人皆有七窍以视听食息，此独无有，尝试凿之。日凿一窍，七日而浑沌死。（《庄子·应帝王》）
（南海之帝是儵，北海之帝是忽，中央之帝是浑沌。儵与忽时常相会于浑沌之地，浑沌待他们很好。儵与忽商量报答浑沌，说：人都有七窍用以视听、饮食、呼吸，唯独浑沌没有，尝试为它开凿出来。于是每天为浑沌开凿一窍，七天之后浑沌死了。）

The king of the South Sea was called Shu, the king of the North Sea was called Hu, and the king of the Central Region was called Chaos. Shu and Hu often met in the territory of Chaos, who treated them very well. They wanted to repay his kindness, and said, "Every man has seven apertures with which to hear, to see, to eat and drink, and to breathe, but Chaos alone has none of them. Let's try and bore some for him." They bored one aperture on Chaos each day, and on the seventh day Chaos died. (*Zhuangzi*)

huófǎ 活法

Literary Flexibility

指诗文创作在遵守规矩法度的同时，又不可死守规矩法度，要有所变化和创新。与拘泥于前人格套、不知变通的"死法"相对立。使作品具备活法的途径，是善于学习前人，在广泛涉猎、融会贯通的基础上，不拘泥、不胶着，从自己的情感和作品的美感出发，使作品的文法、语言呈现崭新的意义。宋代文论家们受到了圆转灵活的禅风影响，在诗文领域倡导活法，使之成为诗文创作的重要原则。

Literary flexibility means that one should respect the rules for writing poetry or prose but not be bound by them; one should encourage change and innovation. The opposite of literary flexibility is literary rigidity under whose influence the writer mechanically imitates the forms of established writers without innovation. One way to attain literary flexibility in one's works is to draw inspiration from others extensively and absorb their talent while refraining from sticking mechanically to the model. One should base oneself on his own feelings and the aesthetic principles so as to create new styles and new ways of expression. Influenced by the Chan spirit of liberal flexibility, literary critics of the Song Dynasty championed flexibility in literary pursuit and established it as an important principle guiding poetry and prose writing.

引例 Citations：

◎学诗当识活法。所谓活法者，规矩备具而能出于规矩之外，变化不测而亦不背于规矩也。是道也，盖有定法而无定法，无定法而有定法。知是者则可以与语活法矣。(刘克庄《后村集》卷二十四引吕本中《〈夏均父集〉序》)
(学作诗要懂得活法。所谓活法，就是作诗的各种规矩法度全都具备而又能跳出规矩法度的限制，使诗文产生各种不可预测的变化而且还不违背规矩。这个道理就是，说有恒定的规矩法度又没有恒定的规矩法度，说没有恒定的规矩法度却又有恒定的规矩法度。懂得这个道理的人，就可以与他谈论活法了。)

Those who wish to learn to write poetry should master literary flexibility. By this I mean that, while knowing all the rules for poetry, the poet goes beyond them to reflect unpredictable changes in his poetry yet without compromising the rules. The principle underlying this way of writing is that there should be set rules, yet they are not fixed; where there seem to be no rules, rules do exist. You can discuss literary flexibility with others only if they understand this principle. (Lü Benzhong: Foreword to *The Collected Poetry of Xia Junfu*)

◎文章一技，要自有活法。若胶古人之陈迹，而不能点化其句语，此乃谓之死法。死法专祖蹈袭，则不能生于吾言之外；活法夺胎换骨，则不能毙于吾言之内。毙吾言者，[故为死法；]生吾言也，故为活法。(俞成《萤雪丛说·文章活法》)
(写文章这种技艺，必须有自己的活法。如果只是拘泥于古人的陈法，而不能将他们的词句化陈出新，这就叫死法。死法只会因袭模仿，不能让我的文章在语言之外获得新生。活法则能超凡脱俗，不会让我的文章被语言困死。文章被语言困死，[所以称死法；] 使文章在语言之外获得新生，所以称活法。）

In writing essays, it is necessary to maintain literary flexibility. If one is bound by the clichés of the classical masters and fails to produce novel ideas, this is what we call literary rigidity. Literary rigidity refers to mechanically copying others without permitting one's own work to acquire new ideas. Literary flexibility, however, allows one's work to free itself from clichés so that the work will not be stifled by stereotyped style of writing. Literary rigidity leads to a literary dead end, while literary flexibility encourages the birth of new ideas by going beyond the limitations of conventional way of writing. (Yu Cheng: *Reflections from Devoted Reading*)

jiān'ài 兼爱

Universal Love

无差等地相互关爱。"兼爱"一说是墨家的基本主张，它所针对的是儒家所提出的爱有差等原则。"兼爱"强调每个人都应像爱自己一样爱他人，像爱自己的家人、国人一样爱别人的家人、爱别国的人，那么人与人之间就会彼此相爱。这种相爱是不分亲疏远近、尊卑上下的，是平等的、没有差别的爱。如果做到兼相爱，就能够避免人与人、家与家、国与国之间的相互攻伐、侵害，进而实现互利。

Universal love, equal affection for all individuals, is a basic concept of the Mohist school of thought, as opposed to the principle of differentiated love advocated by the Confucian school. Universal love emphasizes that you should love others as you love yourself, and love others' relatives and people of other states as you love your own so that all people would love one another equally. This principle of affection has no regard for blood ties or social status. It is an affection that is exercised equally without differentiating between individuals, families, or nations. If such a principle could be realized, we could avoid conflicts between persons, clans, or nations and bring equal benefit to all.

引例 Citation：

◎天下兼相爱则治，交相恶则乱。(《墨子·兼爱上》)
(天下之人彼此相爱则社会安定有序，相互厌恶则社会纷乱不安。)

Universal love will bring peace and order to the world while mutual animosity can only throw the world into disorder. (*Mozi*)

jiěyī-pánbó 解衣盘礴

Sitting with Clothes Unbuttoned and Legs Stretching Out

原指绘画时全神贯注的样子，引申指艺术家进行艺术创作时排除一切外在干扰而进入一种自由任放的精神状态。《庄子·田子方》讲述了一位画师纯任本性、解衣叉腿恣意作画的情形。"解衣"，敞开胸襟，露出胳膊；"盘（一作'般'）礴"，分开双腿，随意坐着，意谓全神贯注于作画。这一术语揭示了率性不拘、自由无待的精神状态是创作优秀艺术作品的重要条件，对于后世书画理论影响很大。

The term originally referred to the appearance of an artist who is concentrating on painting. It has been extended to mean an unrestrained state of mind free from external interruption when an artist is doing creative work. The book *Zhuangzi* describes a painter drawing freely with his clothes thrown open and legs stretching out. "To unbutton one's clothes" is to expose one's chest and arms; and "to sit with legs stretching out" indicates a casual posture while one is concentrating on painting. This term stresses the importance of a relaxed state and complete freedom of mind to the successful creation of quality artwork. This concept had significant influence on subsequent development of theories on calligraphy and painting in later generations.

引例 Citations：

◎宋元君将画图，众史皆至，受揖而立，舐笔和墨，在外者半，有一史后至，儃（tǎn）儃然不趋，受揖不立，因之舍，公使人视之，则解衣般礴，臝。君曰："可矣，是真画者也。"（《庄子·田子方》）

（昔时宋元君准备作画，所有的画师都赶来了，行礼后毕恭毕敬地站着，舐笔调墨，还有一半的人在外面等着。有一个画师来晚了，他悠闲自得，接受了旨意也不恭候站立，随即回到馆舍里去。宋元君派人去看，只见他袒胸露背，叉开腿而坐 [正全神贯注作画]。宋元君说："对呀，这才是真正的画家。"）

Once when King Yuan of the State of Song was to do painting, all the painters came. Half of them, after paying him their respects, stood submissively to prepare brush-pen and ink for him. The other half were waiting outside. One painter, however, arrived late and was casual in manner. After receiving the king's instructions, he returned to his hostel instead of standing there respectfully. The king sent somebody to check on him, and he was seen sitting there painting attentively with his chest and shoulders exposed and both legs stretching out. The king exclaimed, "Yes, that is a real painter!" (*Zhuangzi*)

◎作画须有解衣盘礴、旁若无人意，然后化机在手，元气狼藉，不为先匠所拘，而游于法度之外矣。（恽格《南田画跋·题石谷为王奉常烟客先生画册》）

（绘画必须解开衣襟、叉腿而坐［排除一切外在干扰］，旁若无人，然后手上仿佛握有造化之精微，天地自然之气纵横散布，不再受先前的画匠束缚，而心神驰骋于各种技法之外。）

When doing painting, one should unbutton one's clothes, sit with legs stretching out, keep himself free from all external interruptions, and ignore spectators. That way, one is able to obtain miraculous creative power, draw inspirations from heaven, earth, and nature, go beyond the rules of previous painting masters, and freely use various painting techniques. (Yun Ge: *Nantian's Comments on Paintings*)

jīng（jīngshī）京（京师）

Capital of a Country

　　国都，天子处理政事及所居的城邑。"京"本指高大的山冈、土丘，引申为"大"。"师"即"众"，指人口众多。称天子处理政事及所居的地方为"京"或"京师"，是表明天子都城的规模宏大，也是对天子的尊崇。

This term refers to the place where the Son of Heaven resided and conducted state affairs. *Jing* (京) originally meant a big hill or mound, representing the idea of being big or grand, and *shi* (师) meant a lot of people. To name the place where the the Son of Heaven resided and conducted state affairs *jing* or *jingshi* (京师) suggests that the capital is huge in size and expresses reverence towards the Son of Heaven.

引例 Citation：

◎京师者何？天子之居也。京者何？大也。师者何？众也。天子之居，必以

众大之辞言之。(《公羊传·桓公九年》)

("京师"是什么？是天子居住的地方。"京"指什么？是指规模宏大。"师"指什么？是指人口众多。天子居住的城邑，必须用"众""大"这样的词语来形容。)

What does *jingshi* mean? It is the place where the Son of Heaven resides. What does *jing* mean? It means grandeur and magnificence. What does *shi* mean? It means a lot of people. No words other than populous and grandeur can best describe the place where the Son of Heaven lives. (*Gongyang's Commentary on The Spring and Autumn Annals*)

jīngjì 经济

Govern and Help the People / Economy

治理世事，救助百姓。"经世济民"的略语。"经世"即治理国家和社会事务，使之有条理；"济民"即帮助百姓，使之远离困境。"经济"是中国传统知识分子治学立世的目标和准则之所在，体现了他们学以致用、贡献国家、造福百姓的务实、民本精神。近代以降，"经济"转指创造、转化、实现价值，满足人们物质文化生活需要的社会活动等。

The term is an abbreviation of an expression meaning public governance and support for the people. *Jing* (经) means managing state and social affairs in an orderly manner; *ji* (济) means helping people who are in difficulty. This dual-pronged approach to governance is aimed at making the nation and society prosperous and ensuring that the people live in peace and contentment. The concept of *jingji* (经济) embodies the goals and principles followed by traditional Chinese intellectuals in the pursuit of scholarship and learning, and reflects their commitment to apply learning to the service of the country and for the benefit of the people. In modern times, the term is used to mean "economy," namely, social activities that create, transfer or realize value, and satisfy people's material and cultural needs.

引例 Citations：

◎而国家乃专以辞赋取进士，以墨义取诸科士，皆舍大方而趋小道，虽济济盈庭，求有才有识者十无一二，况天下危困，乏人如此，将何以救之乎？教以经济之业，取以经济之才，庶可救其不逮。（范仲淹《上仁宗答诏条陈十事》）

（朝廷专以诗赋选拔进士，以经义选拔其他科目的士子，都是舍弃了最重要的东西而追逐小技，这样选拔出的人即使济济一堂，但想寻求真有才识的人十个人中找不出一两个。况且天下形势危急，人才如此缺乏，用什么来拯救呢？将经世济民的内容教给士子，用经世济民的才能作为选拔人才的标准，只有这样或可解决人才匮乏的问题。）

The state selects talent through imperial civil service examinations solely on the basis of their literary ability and qualifies scholars only on the basis of their knowledge of the classics. This is ignoring the truly important and choosing the trivial. Even if we have an abundance of candidates, it will be hard to pick one or two competent ones out of every ten. In the current dire situation facing the empire and with paucity of talent, how can we save the country? Only by teaching scholars how to govern and help the people and by selecting talent in those areas can we hope to meet the demand for competent professionals. (Fan Zhongyan: Presentation of Ten Proposals in Response to Emperor Renzong's Proclamation)

◎古来经济才，何事独罕有？（杜甫《上水遣怀》）

（为什么治国安民的人才自古少有？）

Why is it that there have been so few people adept at governance and helping the people since ancient times? (Du Fu: Reflections While Going Upstream)

jīngshì-zhìyòng 经世致用

Study of Ancient Classics Should Meet Present Needs.

学术要对国家和社会的治理发挥实际效用。"经世"即治理国家和社会事务，"致用"即发挥实际效用。17世纪初思想家顾炎武（1613—1682）、王夫之（1619—1692）、黄宗羲（1610—1695）、李颙（yóng，1627—1705）等人倡导学术研究要关注现实，通过解释古代典籍，阐发自己的社会政治见解，解决社会实际问题，以增进国家治理、民生安定、社会改良。这一思想强调知识的政治价值和知识分子的现实担当，体现了中国传统知识分子讲求功效、务实的思想特点和"以天下为己任"的情怀。

Learning should contribute to good governance. *Jingshi* (经世) means governance of the country and society, and *zhiyong* (致用) refers to meeting practical needs. In the early 17th century, thinkers such as Gu Yanwu (1613-1682), Wang Fuzhi (1619-1692), Huang Zongxi (1610-1695), and Li Yong (yóng, 1627-1705) argued that scholarly studies should be geared to meet current needs. They held that while interpreting ancient classics, scholars should expound their views on the social and political issues of their day, solve practical problems, enhance governance of the country, improve people's livelihood, and promote social reform. This view stressed the practical value of knowledge and the practical responsibilities of intellectuals. It reflects the pragmatic character of traditional Chinese intellectuals as well as their concern for the well-being of the people and eagerness to shoulder responsibility for the whole nation.

引例 Citations：

◎凡文之不关于"六经"之指、当世之务者，一切不为。（顾炎武《与人书·三》）

（凡是与"六经"本旨、当世要务无关的文章，一概不作。）

No articles should be written except those that are concerned with what the Six Classics teach us about the current state affairs. (Gu Yanwu: Letters to a Friend)

◎学人贵识时务，《奏议》皆识一时之务者也。……道不虚谈，学贵实效。学而不足以开物成务，康济时艰，真拥衾之妇女耳，亦可羞已！（李颙《二曲集》卷七）

（学者贵在通晓时务，《历代名臣奏议》中的文章都是通晓当时事务的。……道是不可以空谈的，学问贵在讲求实效。学问如果不足以揭示事物真相，确定处理事务的方法，有助于解救时局艰难，那不过是如同拥被自覆不能见人的妇女罢了，实在是可羞愧的呀！）

Scholars should value knowledge of current affairs. Essays in *Memorials to the Throne by Famous Officials Through History* should be about such affairs... There should be no empty talk on abstract theories. The value of knowledge lies in dealing with practical matters. Scholars whose studies do not reveal the essence of things or put forward ways of coping with difficult situations should feel ashamed as an uneducated woman! (Li Yong: *Collected Works of Li Yong*)

◎［先君］益自奋励，自理学及经世致用书，靡不究览。（崔述《先府君行述》）

（先父更加发奋努力，从理学到经世致用的书籍，全都详细研读。）

My late father was very diligent. He read a wide range of works, from Neo-Confucian theories to books on dealing with practical matters. There was nothing he did not study in depth. (Cui Shu: An Account of My Late Father)

jìngjiè 境界

***Jingjie* (Visionary World)**

"境界"本指疆域边界、土地边界，后来在佛经翻译中，"境界"一词被用于精神领域，指人破除对于物质世界的沉迷后所达到的精神层次或修为境域。作为文艺术语，主要指文艺作品中所表现出的审美层次和境域，是作者的创造力、理解力和审美能力在精神层面的综合呈现。有境界的作品是作者真实人格的显现，具备超越凡俗的意味，更能引发读者的共鸣，激发读者的想象，甚至提升读者的感受。"意境"形成较早，而"境界"主要受中唐以后佛教思想的影响而形成。近代学者王国维（1877—1927）《人间词话》对境界的阐释最多。王国维往往将"意境"与"境界"概念通用。他构建了融合西方美学与中国古典美学为一体的"境界论"。但一般说来，意境侧重作者主观寓意与作品形象的完满融会，通过鉴赏使想象得到发挥，而境界则突出心灵感悟使艺术形象得到升华，强调心灵世界对于作品层次的提升。

Jingjie (境界) originally meant border or boundary. Later, it was used to translate the idea of a mental realm in Buddhist sutras, a state of spiritual cultivation achieved after having overcome bewilderment in the material world. As a literary and artistic term, *jingjie* is mainly used to indicate the aesthetic depth in a literary work so as to give full expression to the author's creativity, comprehension, and aesthetic faculties. A work reaching a high level of *jingjie* manifests the author's true personality, transcends the ordinary, strikes a responsive chord in the heart of the reader, stimulates the reader's imagination, and thus enhances the reader's appreciation of his work. The term *yijing* (意境 aesthetic conception) came into being earlier than *jingjie,* which was formed under the influence of Buddhism in the mid-Tang period. In his *Poetic Remarks in the Human World,* modern scholar Wang Guowei (1877-1927) wrote extensively about *jingjie.* He often used *yijing* in the same sense as he used *jingjie* or the other way round. He created the theory of *jingjie,* in which he blended classical Western and classical Chinese aesthetics. Generally speaking, *yijing* refers to a perfect combination of the message the author conveys with the images he uses in his works, and it gives full rein to reader's imagination. The concept of *jingjie,* however, foregrounds the sublimation of artistic images through mental insight, and emphasizes the role of the mental world in elevating the work of art to a higher level.

引例 Citations:

◎山水不出笔墨情景，情景者境界也。(布颜图《画学心法问答》)
(画山水的要素无非就是用笔和墨描绘情与景，情与景融为一体就是境界。)
Painting landscapes is about depicting with brush and ink the artist's affective response to a natural scene. When the artist's sentiments interact intensely with the natural scene, a realm of what we call the visionary world is reached. (Buyantu: How to Paint)

◎言气质，言神韵，不如言境界。有境界，本也；气质、神韵，末也。有境界而二者随之矣。(王国维《〈人间词话〉删稿》)
(与其用气质、神韵做评价标准，不如用境界来评价。境界是根本，气质、神韵是末节。有了境界，气质、神韵必然也就随之出现了。）

The visionary world achieved in literary works serves as a better criterion for making critical evaluation than one's personal character or charm. The visionary world is primary, whereas one's personal character and charm are secondary. Once the visionary world is reached, personal character and charm will naturally follow. (Wang Guowei: *Poetic Remarks in the Human World [The Deleted Part]*)

jìngshēngxiàngwài 境生象外

Aesthetic Conception Transcends Concrete Objects Described.

　　诗文中的审美意境往往在物象之外，需要鉴赏者领悟其中的精神之美。"境"指作品所创造的审美意境，"象"是作品中所呈现出的具体物象。诗歌由语言文字写成，所描写的都是一个个物象，在这些具体的物象之外，能够形成整体的审美情境。唐代诗人刘禹锡（772—842）首次提出这个命题，表达对诗歌意趣的思考，强调文字与物象是确切的，而审美情境却是微妙而难以言传的。在古典诗论意境说的形成过程中，"境生象外"是一个重要的发展阶段。

The aesthetic conception evoked by a poem or prose transcends what a physical object denotes, and a reader needs to perceive and appreciate the beauty of such aesthetic conception. *Jing* (境) here refers to an aesthetic conception created by a poem or prose, while *xiang* (象) refers to the image of a concrete object portrayed in such writing. Composed of words, a poem describes individual objects through which it evokes a coherent poetic conception beyond the physical appearance of such objects. This proposition was first put forward by poet Liu Yuxi (772-842) of the Tang Dynasty to express his understanding of poetry. He pointed out that words and images were concrete while aesthetic conceptions were abstract and subtle and therefore hard to describe. Liu's proposition, namely, aesthetic conception transcending concrete objects described, marked an important stage in the development of the theory of aesthetic conception in classical Chinese poetry.

引例 Citations：

◎夫境象非一，虚实难明，有可睹而不可取，景也；可闻而不可见，风也；虽系乎我形，而妙用无体，心也；义贯众象，而无定质，色也。凡此等，可以偶虚，亦可以偶实。(释皎然《诗议》)

("境"和"象"不是同一个东西，"虚"和"实"也是难以分清。有的可以看到却不能取用，比如景致；有的可以听到却不能看到，比如风；有的虽然与我的形体有关联，而它神奇的应用却不受形体的局限，比如思想；有的其义理贯穿于万物，本身却无固定的形质，比如色彩。所有这些，可以蕴含于"虚写"，也可以蕴含于"实写"。)

Aesthetic conception and imagery are not the same thing, and it is not always easy to distinguish between what is actual and what is implied. Some things like scenery can be seen but not taken, while others such as wind can be heard but not seen. Still others are like thought: it exists in our body but is not restricted by the body. Some pervades everything but possesses no particular shape, like color. All these can be expressed concretely or indirectly by implication. (Shi Jiaoran: *Comments on Poetry*)

◎诗者其文章之蕴耶？义得而言丧，故微而难能。境生于象外，故精而寡和。(刘禹锡《董氏武陵集纪》)

（诗歌难道是高度凝练的文章吗？有文章的意蕴却无需那么多语言，所以非常隐微，很难写得非常好。诗的意境往往产生于所描写的物象之外，所以非常精妙，很少有人能臻于完美。）

Is poetry highly condensed prose? A poem can convey the same meaning of a prose without using many words. Therefore, poetry is implicit and subtle, an art that is hard to master. Poetic conception often transcends what is denoted by the objects described, therefore it is subtle and difficult to achieve. (Liu Yuxi: A Preface to *Dong's Notes from Wuling*)

jū'ān-sīwēi 居安思危

Be on Alert Against Potential Danger When Living in Peace

处在安宁的环境中，要想到可能出现的危难。历代有抱负的统治者都希望国家长治久安，常常提醒自己不要沉湎于安逸享乐，而要勤于政事，励精图治，及时化解社会矛盾，防患于未然。这是一种长远、积极的忧患意识。它不仅成为历代有为的统治阶级时时警醒自己的治政理念，而且也成为现代企业经营的重要指导原则和一般民众积极进取的一种精神。

One should always be on alert against potential danger in time of peace. All ambitious rulers in history hoped to maintain enduring stability. They often reminded themselves not to indulge in pleasure and comfort, but to conduct diligent governance, work hard to make their country prosperous, and resolve social conflicts in a timely manner so as to prevent them from developing into crises. This keen awareness of potential danger was a quality of accomplished rulers in Chinese history. This notion has also become a principle for modern enterprise management, and been adopted by common people in their pursuit of progress .

引例 Citation：

◎若能思其所以危则安矣，思其所以乱则治矣，思其所以亡则存矣。（吴兢《贞观政要·刑法》）

（如果能思考为什么会有危险，国家就安全了；想到为什么会有战乱，国家就太平了；想到为什么会有覆亡，国家就能保存了。）

If one keeps thinking about danger that could emerge, then there can be safety; if one keeps reminding oneself of the possible outbreak of war, then there can be peace; if one keeps thinking about the possible fall of the nation, then the nation can be preserved. (Wu Jing: *Important Political Affairs of the Zhenguan Reign*)

jūn 君

Lord / Nobility / Monarch

最早指包括天子、诸侯、卿、大夫等在内地位尊崇并拥有一定土地、百姓的统治者，后专指诸侯国国君和帝王。"君"的字形由"尹""口"构成，"尹"即治理，指管理国家，治理百姓；"口"即发令。古人认为，为"君"者须具备四个条件：一有"德"，即具备非凡的德行与才能；二有"命"，即秉承"天命"（上天的旨意）；三有"地"，即拥有自己的土地或领地；四有"群"，即管理"群下"（群臣、民众）并为群下所诚心归附。

Originally, the term referred to the Son of Heaven, dukes or princes, ministers, and senior officials who owned land and ruled the common people. It later referred to ducal monarchs and the emperor only. The Chinese character 君 is composed of two parts, namely, 尹 and 口. The top part 尹 means to run a country and govern its people, and the lower part 口 means to give orders. Ancient Chinese believed that a monarch or nobility must possess four qualities: first, having extraordinary virtues and be competent; second, having the mandate of heaven; third, in possession of land or manor; and fourth, having the ability to govern officials and common people, and enjoying their unfailing loyalty.

引例 Citations：

◎天子、诸侯及卿大夫有地者皆曰"君"。(《仪礼·丧服》郑玄注)

(天子、诸侯、卿、大夫，凡拥有自己领地的人，都称作"君"。)

The Son of Heaven, dukes or princes, ministers, and senior officials who own land are all regarded as the nobility or lord. (Zheng Xuan: *Annotations on The Book of Rites and Rituals*)

◎君，群也，下之所归心。(《白虎通义·三纲六纪》)

(君即群，指为群臣、民众所诚心归附。)

The lord, monarch or nobility rules over common people who pledge loyalty to their authority. (*Debates of the White Tiger Hall*)

jūnzǐ 君子

Junzi (Man of Virtue)

"君子"最初用以指称人的社会身份与地位，一般指统治者和贵族男子。

但自孔子（前551—前479）始，"君子"更多地被赋予了道德的意义，德行出众者被称为"君子"，反之为"小人"。在儒家传统中，"君子"成为一种介乎士和圣贤之间的人格理想，它标志着道德人格的确立。"君子"有志于追寻和实践作为价值理想的"道"，并把"道"而不是权力或利益等视为生命意义的根本。

Junzi (君子) was originally used to indicate a person's social status, generally referring to a ruler or a member of the aristocracy. Beginning with Confucius (551-479 BC), the term acquired an additional moral dimension and came to mean someone of true virtue. The opposite of *junzi* is *xiaoren* (小人 petty man), which roughly means the "petty men." In the Confucian tradition, *junzi* is someone who is above a scholar and below a sage in terms of moral influence. A man of virtue pursues and practices the ideal known as Dao and regards Dao as the fundamental meaning of life above power or gains.

引例 Citations：

◎君子喻于义，小人喻于利。(《论语·里仁》)
（君子知晓并遵循义，小人知晓并追逐利。）

A man of virtue understands and observes what is morally right; while a petty man only has his eyes on and goes after what brings personal gains. (*The Analects*)

◎君子，成德之名。(朱熹《论语集注》卷一)
（君子是对道德成就者的称谓。）

A man of virtue is someone who has achieved moral integrity. (Zhu Xi: *The Analects Variorum*)

kāiwù-chéngwù 开物成务

Understand Things and Succeed in One's Endeavors

揭示事物的真相并据以做成事情。"开物"即揭开事物真相，弄清事物的内在联系和规律；"成务"即根据事物的内在联系和规律，确定适当方法，把事情做好做成。这是古人从《周易》的变化规律及社会功用中所悟出的认识世界、改造世界、服务自身的思想方法和行动纲领，蕴含着朴素的科学精神。

This term means to find out the truth of things, and act accordingly to succeed in what one does. *Kaiwu* (开物) means to reveal the truth of things and understand their intrinsic relations and rules. *Chengwu* (成务) means to use proper methods to do things successfully according to their intrinsic relations and rules. This was a perception and guide to action that the ancient Chinese learned from *The Book of Changes* and everyday life, which they used to understand the world, change the world, and serve themselves. This concept represents a fundamental principle of social science.

引例 **Citation**：

◎夫《易》，开物成务，冒天下之道，如斯而已者也。(《周易·系辞上》)
(《易》这本书，旨在揭示万物真相，确定行事原则并做好事情，总括天下万物的基本法则，如此而已。)

The Book of Changes aims to reveal the truth of all things on earth, point out how to handle affairs, and do them right. It covers the basic rules governing all things on earth. (*The Book of Changes*)

kūn 坤

Kun (The Earth Symbol)

"八卦"之一，由三个"阴爻"组成，画为"☷"。又为"六十四卦"之一，由六个"阴爻"组成，画为"䷁"。按照易学的解释，由于"坤"卦全部由"阴爻"组成，因此具有纯"阴"之性，被用以象征各种"阴"性的事物或原则。"坤"卦的基本象征意义是地，在社会领域主要象征女性、母亲、臣民等社会角色以及柔顺宽厚的行事原则。结合"坤"卦的各种象征意义，"坤"还被赋予了创生、长养万物之义。

One of the eight trigrams, *kun*(坤) consists of three yin lines: ☷. It is also one of the 64 hexagrams when it consists of six yin lines: ䷁. According to scholars on *The Book of Changes,* as the *kun* trigram is composed only of yin lines, it is purely yin and is thus used to symbolize all yin things or principles. The *kun* trigram symbolizes earth, and when it comes to society, it symbolizes the social roles played the by the female, the mother, and the subjects of the ruler, as well as gentle, kind, and generous ways of doing things. In this context, *kun* also means creating and nourishing all things under heaven.

引例 Citations：

◎坤，顺也。(《周易·说卦》)

(坤，意为柔顺。)

The *kun* trigram means gentleness. (*The Book of Changes*)

◎至哉坤元，万物资生，乃顺承天。(《周易·彖上》)

(伟大的坤元，万物依赖它才得以发生，它顺承着天道。)

Great is the *kun* hexagram! All things owe their existence to *kun*, since it represents the way of heaven. (*The Book of Changes*)

礼

Li (Rites / Social Norms / Propriety)

社会秩序的总称，用以规范个人与他人、与天地万物乃至鬼神之间的关系。"礼"通过各种有关器物、仪式、制度的规定，明确了个人特定的身份及相应的责任、权力，从而区别了个人在社会群体中长幼、亲疏、尊卑的差等。"礼"以这样的区别来实现对个体的安顿，并由此达成人与人、人与天地万物之间的和谐。

Li (礼) is a general term for social norms which regulate an individual's relationship with other people, everything else in nature, and even ghosts and spirits. By setting various regulations about ceremonial vessels, rituals, and systems, rites define an individual's specific status and corresponding duty and power, thereby differentiating between people in a community in terms of age, kinship, and social status. With such differentiations, the rites determine the proper position of each individual, thus achieving harmony among human beings, and between humanity and everything else in nature.

引例 Citations：

◎夫礼，天之经也，地之义也，民之行也。(《左传·昭公二十五年》)

（礼是天地运行的法则，民众行为的规范。）

Rites are the rules governing the movement of heaven and earth as well as code of conduct for the people. (*Zuo's Commentary on The Spring and Autumn Annals*)

◎夫礼者，所以定亲疏、决嫌疑、别同异、明是非也。(《礼记·曲礼上》)
(礼是确定亲疏关系、决断疑惑之事、区别同异、辨明是非的依据。)

Rites are the basis for determining proper human relations, clarifying ambiguities, differentiating between things, and telling right from wrong. (*The Book of Rites*)

◎礼之用，和为贵。先王之道斯为美，小大由之。有所不行，知和而和，不以礼节之，亦不可行也。(《论语·学而》)
(礼的应用，以和谐为贵。古代君主的治国方法，可宝贵的地方就在这里，不论大事小事都依照"和"的原则去做。也有行不通的时候，如果仍一味为了和谐而和谐，而不用礼来加以节制，也是不可行的。)

Make harmony a top priority in the application of rites. That is a key feature that characterizes governance by sovereign rulers in ancient past. Always act upon the rule of harmony, no matter whether the issue at hand is minor or major. Sometimes, however, this rule may fail to work. If one insists on seeking harmony just for the sake of harmony instead of qualifying it with rites, then there will be no hope to succeed. (*The Analects*)

miàowù 妙悟

Subtle Insight

　　一种特定情境下形成的心理体验状态，在精神自由放松的状态下，直接领会、感知美，然后呈现于诗歌作品中，从而使诗歌整体的美感超越具体的语言文字，达到极高的审美层次。它能够在瞬间的心理体验中，达到物我两忘的境界，领悟诗歌的本质和永恒的精神之美。在佛、道、玄三家的义理中，"妙"指思维方面的精微玄奥，而"悟"则是一种体验式的、不依赖逻辑推理的认识方式。禅宗提倡通过禅修来达到本心清净、空灵清澈的精神境界，这种境界与文艺审美的精神境界有着密切的联系。南宋严羽（？—1264）《沧浪诗话》借用禅宗的思想，对"妙悟"在诗歌创作中的特征与功用作了充分的阐发，开创以禅喻诗的先河，影响较大。"妙悟"也影响了中国古代的绘画与书法。

This term refers to an inner experience one gains under special circumstances. When the mind is so relaxed and peaceful, it allows one to develop an intimate appreciation and understanding of beauty and then express it in a poem. The beauty of the poem thus inspired transcends words and creates an intense aesthetic experience. Subtle insight enables the reader to appreciate the essence and lasting beauty of a poem by creating a spontaneous experience so engrossing that one becomes oblivious to both himself and the outside world. According to Buddhist, Daoist, and Metaphysical principles, "subtle" refers to the minute and profound nature of thinking, whereas "insight" is an intensely personal experience derived not from logical reasoning. Chan Buddhism promotes meditation as a way to return to the mind's original tranquility and thus achieve a clear and simple state of mind. Such a state of mind comes from literary and artistic experience. In *Canglang's Criticism on Poetry*, literary critic Yan Yu (?-1264) of the Southern Song Dynasty dealt extensively with the function and features of subtle insight in poetry writing by drawing on Chan philosophy. This book is the first one to apply Chan terms to critical writing on poetry and has thus gained great influence. The concept of subtle insight has also influenced traditional painting and calligraphy in China.

引例 Citations：

◎ 凝神遐想，妙悟自然，物我两忘，离形去智。（张彦远《历代名画记》卷二）

（凝聚心神，自由畅想，对自然之美的体悟达到绝妙境地，忘记了外在世界，也忘记了自身，脱离形体的束缚，抛弃知识的局限。）

By concentrating one's mind and freeing one's thoughts, one can reach such a fascinating state in appreciating the beauty of nature as to become oblivious to the outside world and one's own self, totally free from the constraints of physical forms and limitations of knowledge. (Zhang Yanyuan: *Famous Paintings Through History*)

◎ 大抵禅道惟在妙悟，诗道亦在妙悟。且孟襄阳学力下韩退之远甚，而其诗独出退之之上者，一味妙悟而已。（严羽《沧浪诗话·诗辨》）

（一般说来禅修最重要的原则是妙悟，作诗最重要的原则也是妙悟。比如孟浩然的学问才力远远比不上韩愈，但是孟浩然的诗却比韩愈水平高，就是因为他一心妙悟。）

Generally speaking, the most important principle of meditation is to achieve subtle insight, and this is the most important principle underlying poetry writing as well. For example, while Meng Haoran is no equal to Han Yu in terms of knowledge and talent, his poems surpass those of Han Yu because he is able to create subtle insight. (Yan Yu: *Canglang's Criticism on Poetry*)

mínbāo-wùyǔ 民胞物与

All People Are My Brothers and Sisters, and All Things Are My Companions.

世人都是我的同胞，万物都是我的同伴。北宋张载（1020—1077）认为人和万物都是天地自然之气化生的，本性相同，因此提出"民胞物与"，主张爱世上一切人和物。这一思想超越了以人类为中心的窠臼，达到了人我、物我的统一与和谐，与"厚德载物"的内在精神是一致的，是宋明理学思想的重要组成部分。

This idea was first put forward by Zhang Zai (1020-1077) of the Northern Song Dynasty, who held that people and things are all created by the vital force of heaven and earth, and thus are similar in nature. He advocated love for all people and things in the world, and his view transcended the old anthropocentric viewpoint and aimed to reach harmony between oneself and other human beings as well as between oneself and other creatures and things. It is the same as the idea that a true gentleman has ample virtue and cares for all things. This notion is an important part of the School of Principle of the Song and Ming dynasties.

引例 Citation：

◎故天地之塞，吾其体；天地之帅，吾其性。民，吾同胞；物，吾与也。（张载《西铭》）

（所以，充塞天地的[气]构成了我的形体；支配天地的[道]构成了我的本性。世人都是我的同胞，万物都是我的同伴。）

Therefore, what fills heaven and earth constitutes my body; what governs heaven and earth forms my nature. All people are my brothers and sisters, and all things are my companions. (Zhang Zai: The Western Inscription)

míngshí 名实

Name and Substance

"实"指实存的事物,"名"指赋予事物的名号、称谓。"名"建立在"实"的基础之上,不能脱离对"实"的认识。"名"体现着人们对事物的本质及其相互关系的理解和设计。人们通过命名的方式,将万事万物纳入到一定的秩序之中。事物依据其被赋予的名号、称谓,在有秩序的整体中确立自己的地位和意义。

Shi (实) refers to an existing object, while *ming* (名) refers to a name, a title or an appellation given to an object. A name is given on the basis of substance, and it cannot be separated from the knowledge of the substance. Names give expression to people's understanding about the essence of objects and their interrelations, and the way in which they handle such interrelations. By giving names, people integrate all things and all objects into a certain order. The position and significance of an object in the whole system are determined on the basis of the name, title or the appellation given to it.

引例 Citations：

◎所以谓,名也。所谓,实也。(《墨子·经说上》)

(对实物的称谓就是"名",所指称的对象就是"实"。)

That by which an object is called is the name. That which a name refers to is a substance. (*Mozi*)

◎物固有形，形固有名，此言不得过实，实不得延名。(《管子·心术上》)
（事物固有其形态，形态固有其名称，因此称说的名不能超过实，实不能延伸于名称所指之外。）

An object has a shape, and a shape has a name. The name must not go beyond the substance, and the substance must not extend beyond its name. (*Guanzi*)

mìng 命

Mandate / Destiny

最初指"天命"，即上天对人事的命令。上天根据人的德行状况对人施与奖赏或惩罚。"天命"决定着王朝的更替、国家的兴衰乃至个人的吉凶祸福，被认为是一种不可抗拒的力量。后人逐渐淡化了"命"与"天"的关联，侧重于强调"命"的不可抗拒之义，也即是命运。对人而言，"命"意味着来自于外部的某种限制，标志着人力的极限，并在某种意义上体现为人的无可奈何的处境。

The earliest meaning of the term was mandate of heaven, that is, the intentions and instructions that Heaven expressed to humans. The implication was that Heaven meted out rewards and punishments on human beings as their moral conduct deserved. The mandate of Heaven was considered an irresistible force that determined dynastic changes, the rise and fall of nations, and even the fate of ordinary people. Later, the link with Heaven became weaker; instead, the unavoidable destiny or fate prevailed. For human beings, the term implies the external limits that determine what is possible and what is not. In one sense, it expresses the helplessness of human beings.

引例 Citations:

◎天命靡常。(《诗经·大雅·文王》)
(上天的命令没有恒常不变的。)

Heaven-bestowed supreme power is not eternal. (*The Book of Songs*)

◎知其不可奈何而安之若命。(《庄子·人间世》)
(知道没有办法可以改变,故安然处之顺应其命。)

Knowing that one cannot change his destiny, one should face things calmly and submit himself to fate. (*Zhuangzi*)

qìxiàng 气象

Prevailing Features

原是自然界中景色物候的总称,也指某个时期社会的总体精神风貌。"气象"兼指气概、气势和景色、景物两方面而言。具体到艺术领域,指艺术作品所呈现出的风格与气概,内涵偏重于宏伟壮大,多用"雄浑""浑厚""峥嵘"等来修饰。唐代文论家们开始用"气象"一词来论述诗歌、文章的神采和风貌。从宋代起,"气象"成为文论的重要概念,用以品评诗歌、文章以及书画作品的风格与气概。"气象"往往反映特定文艺时期的精神风貌,例如盛唐气象实即盛唐时代的诗歌风貌,也与创作者个人的襟抱气度相关。

Qixiang (气象), originally a term about the general state of scenery and physical objects in nature, also refers to the prevailing features of a society in a given period of time. This description carries the meaning of great appeal and impact as well as scenery and objects. When applied to art, it refers to the overall style and appeal in a piece of artistic work. It connotes grandeur and magnificence, and is often used in conjunction with such words as "heroic," "immense," and "sublime." Literary critics of the Tang Dynasty began using the term to comment on the style and features of a poem or an essay. Since the Song Dynasty, the term has become an important concept in literary criticism, used to critique the style and artistic flair of poems, essays, calligraphy, and paintings. It is often thought to reflect the prevailing features in literature and art of a particular period. For instance, during the prime of the Tang Dynasty, the term referred to the appeal of both poems and the poets who wrote them.

引例 Citations：

◎盛唐诸公之诗，如颜鲁公书，既笔力雄壮，又气象浑厚。（严羽《答出继叔临安吴景仙书》）

（盛唐诸多诗人的诗作，好比颜真卿的书法作品一样，笔力既雄壮感人，气象又质朴厚重。）

Works of many poets during the prime of the Tang Dynasty struck readers with their powerful expression, just like the calligraphy of Yan Zhenqing. (Yan Yu: Letter in Reply to Uncle Wu Jingxian in Lin'an)

◎大凡为文当使气象峥嵘，五色绚烂，渐老渐熟，及造平淡。（周紫芝《竹坡诗话》引苏轼语）

（一般说来，写文章应该做到气象高峻壮美，语言文采绚丽。随着作者年龄增长、阅历丰富及风格逐渐成熟，最终归于平淡自然。）

Generally speaking, one should strive to achieve an elegant style and powerful expression in writing. However, as a writer becomes more experienced, his writing will grow simple and natural in style. (Su Shi, as quoted in Zhou Zizhi: *Zhupo's Remarks on Poetry*)

◎五言律体……唯工部诸作气象嵬（wéi）峨，规模宏远。（胡应麟《诗薮·内编四》）

（就五言律诗而言……只有杜甫的作品气象高峻不凡，格局广阔深远。）

Regarding five-character-a-line verses … only Du Fu's poems possess a style that is imposing and original and a quality that is both profound and forceful. (Hu Yinglin: *An In-depth Exploration of Poetry*)

qián 乾

Qian

"八卦"之一，由三个"阳爻"组成，画为"☰"。又为"六十四卦"之一，由六个"阳爻"组成，画为"䷀"。按照易学的解释，由于"乾"卦全部由阳爻组成，因此具有纯阳之性，被用以象征各种阳性的事物或原则。"乾"卦的基本象征意义是天，在社会领域主要象征男性、父亲、君主等社会角色以及刚健有为的行事原则。结合"乾"卦的各种象征意义，"乾"还被赋予了创生、统领万物之义。

One of the eight trigrams, it consists of three yang lines: ☰. It is also one of the 64 hexagrams when it consists of six yang lines: ䷀. According to scholars on *The Book of Changes*, as the *qian* trigram is composed only of yang lines, it is purely yang and is thus used to symbolize all yang things or principles. The *qian* trigram symbolizes heaven, and in social terms, it symbolizes the social roles played by the male, the father, and the monarch, as well as decisive and vigorous ways of doing things. In this context, *qian* also means creating and leading all things under heaven.

引例 Citations：

◎乾，健也。(《周易·说卦》)

(乾，意为刚健有为。)

The *qian* trigram symbolizes vigor and vitality. (*The Book of Changes*)

◎大哉乾元，万物资始，乃统天。(《周易·彖上》)

(伟大的乾元，万物依赖它开始产生，乾元统帅天的运行与效用。)

Great is the *qian* hexagram! All things owe their existence to it, and it guides the movement of heaven and creates its impact. (*The Book of Changes*)

qǔjìng 取境

Qujing (Conceptualize an Aesthetic Feeling)

指诗人在诗歌创作中，选取最能表达内心情感的物象并构思符合诗人自己的审美感受的意境。由唐代诗僧皎然（720—796？）在《诗式》中提出。皎然在总结六朝至中唐诗人的创作经验与方式时提出，作诗的时候，要精于构思，立意尽量奇特，不落俗套，在一番苦思冥想之后，灵感迸发、神完气足，才能写出境界上好的诗歌作品。虽然构思险奇，但是最终形成的作品风格要平易自然，不要显露精心思索的痕迹。取境与意境、境界等术语关系密切，属于中国古典诗论中关于"境"的术语系列。

The term means to conceptualize an aesthetic feeling by selecting images that best express a poet's sentiments and appreciation. The term *qujing* (取境) was coined by the Tang monk poet Jiaoran (720-796?) in his *Poetic Styles*. After conducting a review of how poets from the Six Dynasties to the mid-Tang Dynasty wrote poems, he concluded that to write poems, one must structure one's thoughts ingeniously so as to generate a uniquely original conception with no trace of clichés. Then, after some deep thinking, an inspiration will arise and his imagination will run free. In this way, the poet can create a poem with a fine visionary world. Although the conception may be highly original, ultimately the style of the work should be simple and natural without any traces of having been laboriously crafted. This term is closely related to the terms *jingjie* (境界) and *yijing* (意境); together, they are part of a series of terms dealing with *jing* (境) in classical Chinese poetics.

引例 Citations：

◎夫诗人之思，初发取境偏高，则一首举体便高；取境偏逸，则一首举体便逸。(释皎然《诗式·辩体有一十九字》)
(诗人刚开始构思的时候，如果取境偏于高迈，那么整首诗的意境就高迈；如果取境偏于飘逸，那么整首诗的意境就飘逸。)

When the poet starts to compose a poem, if his conception of the poem tends towards grandeur, then the artistic conception of the poem will be grand; if his conception of the poem is free and easy, so will the aesthetic conception of the poem be. (Shi Jiaoran: *Poetic Styles*)

◎夫不入虎穴，焉得虎子。取境之时，须至难至险，始见奇句。成篇之后，观其气貌，有似等闲不思而得，此高手也。(释皎然《诗式·取境》)
(不进入老虎的洞穴，就抓不住老虎的幼崽。作诗取境的时候，必须从最难最险的地方开始构思，才能创作出奇妙的诗句。全篇完成之后，再看整首诗的气势和面貌，似乎很平常像没经过思索就写成了，这才是作诗的高手。）

Without entering the tiger's den, one cannot catch a cub. When developing one's poetic conception, it is necessary to begin to contemplate what is most difficult and daring before great lines can spring to mind. After one completes a poem, one should review its overall structure and appeal. If it looks so smooth and natural as if written effortlessly, then it will be a great poem. (Shi Jiaoran: *Poetic Styles*)

réndào 人道

Way of Man

为人之道，指人类社会必须遵循的行为规范（与"天道"相对），也是人类社会得以维持和运行的关系及法则。近代以后，西学东渐，它演变为以尊重和关爱人的生命、幸福、尊严、自由、个性发展等为原则的行为规范和权利。

The way of man refers to the code of conduct that people must observe and also the relations and norms that keep human society on the right track. The way of man stands in contrast to the way of heaven. When Western culture was introduced to China in modern times, the term gained the meaning of respect and care for people's lives, well-being, dignity, freedom, and individuality.

引例 Citations：

◎天道远，人道迩。（《左传·昭公十八年》）

(天之道遥远，人事之道切近。)

The way of heaven is far away; the way of man is near. (*Zuo's Commentary on The Spring and Autumn Annals*)

◎尧、舜不易日月而兴，桀、纣不易星辰而亡，天道不改而人道易也。（陆贾《新语·明诚》）

(尧、舜没有改变日月的运行而兴起，桀、纣也没有改变日月的运行而灭亡，这是因为天道没有改变而人道改变的缘故。)

The rise of Yao and Shun did not change the sun and the moon. The fall of Jie and Zhou did not change the stars. This is because the way of man does not change the way of heaven. (Lu Jia: *New Thoughts*)

rénwén 人文

Renwen (Human Culture)

指礼乐教化、典章制度，即诗书、礼乐、法度等精神文明的创造以及与之相关的既有差等又有调和的社会秩序。与"天文"（日月星辰等天体的运行状态和规律）相对。也泛指人事，即人类社会的行为、习俗或状态。近代以后，受西学影响，"人文"演变指人类社会的各种文化现象，研究人类社会文化现象的学科称为人文科学。

Renwen (人文) encompasses the cultural and ethical progress created by rites, music, education, codes, and systems as well as a social order which is hierarchical but harmonious. *Renwen* is in contrast to *tianwen* (天文), the study of celestial bodies including the sun, moon, and stars. *Renwen* also refers to human affairs in general, that is, behaviors, customs, and the human state.

Under the influence of Western culture in the modern period, *renwen* came to mean cultural phenomena in human society as well as the humanities, which are academic disciplines that study human culture.

引例 Citations：

◎观乎天文，以察时变；观乎人文，以化成天下。(《周易·彖上》)

(观察日月星辰的运行状态，可以知道四季的变换；考察诗书礼乐的发展状况，可以用来教化天下百姓，实现文治昌明。)

By observing the movement of constellations, we can learn about the change of seasons; by observing development of human culture, we can enlighten the people and build a civilized society. (*The Book of Changes*)

◎夫玄象著明，以察时变，天文也；圣达立言，化成天下，人文也。达幽显之情，明天人之际，其在文乎？(《北齐书·文苑传序》)

(日月星辰等运行昭著，人们以此推断时事的变化，这就是"天文"；贤圣通达之人著书立说，教导民众向善，实现文治昌明，这就是"人文"。通晓无形与有形的实情，弄懂上天与人事的微妙联系，恐怕就在于"文"吧？)

When the movement of celestial bodies is manifest, we can infer from it changes of the times, which is about the distribution and movement of celestial bodies as well as climate change. When sages disseminate their vision in writing to educate the people and build a thriving, prosperous, and refined society, that is about human culture. To learn about the actual state of the visible and the invisible and the subtle relations between heaven and humans, it is essential to study both natural phenomena and human culture. (*The History of the Northern Qi Dynasty*)

sānxuán 三玄

Three Metaphysical Classics

《老子》《庄子》《周易》三部著作的合称。汉代五经之学盛行，魏晋时期思想大变，《老子》《庄子》《周易》为学者所关注。经由何晏（？—249）、王弼（226—249）、向秀（227？—272）、郭象（？—312）等人的注解，这些经典被赋予了新的意义。"三玄"既是魏晋名士清谈的中心内容，也是玄学家借以发挥自己哲学思想的基本素材。"三玄"之学集中探讨了个体生命与外在世界之间的矛盾，也充分展现了儒家和道家思想之间的冲突与互补。

The term refers to three metaphysical works: *Laozi*, *Zhuangzi*, and *The Book of Changes*. During the Han Dynasty, the study of the Five Classics was the prevailing trend; but during the Wei and Jin dynasties, the way of thinking changed considerably. Scholars turned their attention to *Laozi*, *Zhuangzi*, and *The Book of Changes*. The annotations by such people as He Yan (?-249), Wang Bi (226-249), Xiang Xiu (227?-272), and Guo Xiang (?-312) gave these classics new meanings. The Three Metaphysical Classics were the focus of discourse among leading scholars of the Wei and Jin dynasties, and they were regarded by scholars of metaphysic learning as a source of inspiration when they expressed their philosophical thinking. The study of the Three Metaphysical Classics focused on probing the contradiction between individual life and the outside world. It also fully demonstrated conflict and complementarity between the thinking of Confucian and Daoist scholars.

引例 Citation：

◎洎(jì)于梁世，兹风复阐，《庄》《老》《周易》，总谓"三玄"。（颜之推《颜氏家训·勉学》）

（到了梁代，这一风气再次获得阐扬，《庄子》《老子》《周易》三部著作，总称为"三玄"。）

In the Liang Dynasty, there was a renewed interest in the study of *Zhuangzi*, *Laozi*, and *The Book of Changes*, which were collectively referred to as the Three Metaphysical Classics. (Yan Zhitui: *Admonitions for the Yan Clan*)

shàngdì 上帝

Supreme Ruler / Ruler of Heaven

主要含义有二：其一，上古传说中指主宰宇宙万事万物的最高天神。也叫"天帝"。商周时期，巫是联通人与上帝的媒介，巫通过卜筮向上帝请示，传达上帝的旨意。其二，指帝国或王朝的最高统治者，即帝王、君主，包括远古或死去的帝王、君主，犹言"天子"。基督教传入中国后，基督教教士又借用"上帝"一词作为对其所崇奉之神 God 的译称。

The term has two meanings. One is the supreme ruler of the universe, also known as the Ruler of Heaven. During the Shang and Zhou dynasties, wizards were the intermediaries between humans and the supreme ruler. They asked for his orders by means of divination and conveyed them to humans. The other meaning is the supreme ruler of an empire or dynasty, that is, the emperor or monarch, including those of remote antiquity and those who had died; each was referred to as Son of Heaven. After Christianity was introduced to China, missionaries used this term as a translation of the word "God."

引例 Citations：

◎先王以作乐崇德，殷荐之上帝，以配祖考。(《周易·象上》)
(先代的君王因此制作音乐，赞美功德，以盛大的典礼奉献给上帝，并让祖先的神灵配祭。)

Former kings thus created music to extol virtue, conducted grand ceremonies to honor the Ruler of Heaven, and worshipped ancestral tablets. (*The Book of Changes*)

◎皇矣上帝，临下有赫。监观四方，求民之莫。(《诗经·大雅·皇矣》)
(伟大的上帝呀，俯察人间好分明。洞察天下四方地，努力寻求民安定。)

August is the Ruler of Heaven, beholding the mortal world in majesty. He surveys and watches the four quarters, bringing peace and stability to the people. (*The Book of Songs*)

shàngshàn-ruòshuǐ 上善若水

Great Virtue Is Like Water.

最完美的善就像水的品性一样，滋润万物却不与万物相争。出自《老子》。老子以水的这种柔弱之性比喻至善的执政者应有的品德。执政者面对百姓，应如水之于万物，辅助、成就百姓的自然而不与百姓相争。后多指为人处世时能像水一样滋润万物，尽己所能帮助他人却从不争名逐利，或者具有坚忍负重、谦卑居下的品格。

The greatest virtue is just like water, nurturing all things without competing with them. This term was first used by Laozi to advocate the belief that a virtuous ruler should govern with gentle and accommodating qualities as demonstrated by water. He should assist and provide for people just like what the water does, instead of competing with them for resources. Later, this term came to mean that people should nourish all things as water does and try their best to help people without seeking fame or profit. It also refers to human virtues such as endurance for the sake of achieving a noble goal and modesty.

引例 Citation：

◎上善若水。水善利万物而不争，处众人之所恶（wù），故几于道。(《老子·八章》)

(至善之人具有如水一般的品德。水善于滋润万物而不与万物相争，处于众人所厌恶的卑下之处，因此水几近于道。)

Great virtue is like water. Water nourishes all things gently and does not compete with anything, content to be in a low place not sought by people. Water is therefore closest to Dao. (*Laozi*)

shényǔwùyóu 神与物游

Interaction Between the Mind and the Subject Matter

文艺创作中人的精神与外物交融、自由驰骋的构思活动。在这一构思活动中，一方面人的精神感觉和想象投射到客观事物上，使客观事物具有了审美色彩；另一方面，虚无缥缈的精神感觉和想象也借助客观事物得以表达和呈现。"神"与"物"的自由融合，超越了时间与空间的限制，形成艺术形象，然后经过语言的表现，产生了美妙的文艺作品。这一术语源自《庄子》的"乘物以游心"，后经南朝刘勰（465？—520）《文心雕龙》的系统阐发，成为对"神思"这一术语的概括性论述，突出艺术构思过程中心灵与物象交融、自由想象的特点，既说明了艺术创作中的构思活动，也高度概括了文艺创作中的审美心理与创作自由的特点。

This term refers to the creative process through which a writer interacts with subject matter and gives free rein to his imagination. During the process, he projects onto real objects his mental sensations and imaginings, and endows them with an aesthetic tone. Conversely, his imaginary sensations and imaginings are given concrete expression by real objects. The free interaction between mind and subject matter, transcending the limitations of space and time, creates a superb artistic work depicted in language. The term originated in the words of "taking advantage of the circumstances to let your mind wander freely" in *Zhuangzi*. Later, this idea was systematically developed by Liu Xie (465?-520) in *The Literary Mind and the Carving of Dragons* during the Southern Dynasties to describe imaginative contemplation. The term stresses the importance of interaction between the mind and the poetic subject matter as well as free imagination in the process of artistic creation. It demonstrates the process of thinking in artistic creation and succinctly summarizes the underlying features of aesthetic appreciation and freedom in artistic creation.

引例 Citations：

◎其始也，皆收视反听，耽思傍讯。精骛八极，心游万仞。其致也，情曈昽（tónglóng）而弥鲜，物昭晰而互进。（陆机《文赋》）
（在开始写文章时，必须停止一切视听活动，凝聚心神，广为求索，精神奔驰于八方极远之地，心灵飞翔至万仞极高之境。到极致时，情感由朦胧而渐趋明朗，物象也随之清晰而在眼前交替呈现。）

When starting to write an essay, one should keep away sounds and sights and keep his mind focused so as to allow the imagination to search freely in the universe. When his mind reaches the farthest end, all confusion will dissipate, and images will clearly emerge in his mind one after another. (Lu Ji: The Art of Writing)

◎故思理为妙，神与物游。神居胸臆，而志气统其关键；物沿耳目，而辞令管其枢机。（刘勰《文心雕龙·神思》）

（所以写作构思的奇妙之处，可以使思绪和想象与外在事物自由地连接交融。思绪和想象蕴藏于内心，由人的情志、气质主宰；外物通过听觉、视觉来认识，而将其表达出来却是由言辞负责的。）

What is marvelous about composing a poem is that it makes it possible for the mind and the imagination to interact freely with external objects. The feelings and imaginings that well up from within are determined by a writer's aspirations and temperament. We recognize external objects through hearing and vision, but these objects are expressed through the use of language. (Liu Xie: *The Literary Mind and the Carving of Dragons*)

shényùn 神韵

Elegant Subtlety

指文学艺术作品中清远淡雅的意蕴和韵味。原本是对人物的风度神情的评价，魏晋时人认为人格之美在于内在精神气韵，不同于汉代人推重外形。后来这一概念进入书画理论，指作品内在的精神韵味。明代人从书画理论引入诗歌理论，使神韵成为对诗歌风格的要求，清代王士禛（1634—1711）是"神韵说"的发扬光大者，他特意编选了《唐诗神韵集》，借编选理想的诗歌阐发自己的审美趣味，又在诗歌理论著作中大力倡导，构建起独具特色的诗歌艺术审美体系，从而使"神韵说"得以完善定型，最终成为清代诗学的一大流派。

This term refers to the subtle elegance of literary and artistic works. It was originally used to depict a person's mien and manner. During the Wei and Jin dynasties, the propriety inherent in a person was valued, whereas during the previous Han Dynasty, a person's external appearance was stressed. Later on, this concept was incorporated into the theory of calligraphy and painting to refer to the elegant subtlety of a work. In the Ming Dynasty, the concept was extended to the theory of poetry, and elegant subtlety became a requirement for composing poetry. Later, Wang Shizhen (1634-1711) of the Qing Dynasty further developed the theory of elegant subtlety. In compiling *The Elegant Subtlety of the Tang Poetry*, he elaborated on his aesthetic views. In his writings on poetry theory, Wang Shizhen championed these views and created his own unique poetical aesthetics, enriching the theory of elegant subtlety, and making it a major school of the Qing-dynasty poetics.

引例 Citations：

◎诗之佳，拂拂如风，洋洋如水，一往神韵，行乎其间。（陆时雍《诗镜·总论》）

（好诗如同拂面的清风，如同流过的浩大河水，仿佛有种神韵行进在诗的字里行间。）

Just as gentle breeze touching one's face and the river flowing past, a good poem has elegant subtlety permeating its lines. (Lu Shiyong: *A Comprehensive*

Digest of Good Ancient Poems)

◎予尝观唐末五代诗人之作，卑下嵬（wéi）琐，不复自振，非惟无开元、元和作者豪放之格，至神韵兴象之妙以视陈隋之季，盖百不及一焉。（王士禛《〈梅氏诗略〉序》）

（我曾经读唐末五代时的诗人作品，格调卑下猥琐，气势不振，非但没有开元、元和年间诗作的豪放风格，在神韵、兴象的绝妙方面，甚至连陈、隋衰微时期的诗作的百分之一都比不上。）

I have read the works by poets of the late Tang Dynasty and the Five Dynasties and found their poetry mean-spirited, trivial, and depressed. They were far less bold and daring than those poems written between the Kaiyuan and Yuanhe periods of the Tang Dynasty. Worse still, they did not have the slightest traces of the elegant subtlety and inspiring imagery that were evident in the poetry written in the State of Chen during the Northern Dynasties and in the Sui Dynasty when poetry was already in decline. (Wang Shizhen: Foreword to *Poetry by the Mei Family*)

shīchū-yǒumíng 师出有名

Fighting a War with a Moral Justification

兴兵开战要有正当的名义或理由。泛指做事有正当的理由。它包含两层意思：其一，师直为壮，谓出兵理由正当，则士气旺盛，战斗力强，否则难以服众；其二，无故不得兴兵，防止因贪、怒而穷兵黩武。其核心在于强调战争的正义性。这是文明精神的体现。

To wage a war, one must have a legitimate cause, just as we ought to have such a reason in doing all things. The term has two meanings. The first is that moral justification is a source of strength when waging a war. With moral justification, the troops will have high morale and strength in fighting. Without it, it would be difficult to command the troops. The second meaning is that war must not be waged without a just cause. Greed or anger should not be allowed to lead to militarism and aggression. The underlying notion of this concept is that war can only be fought with a just cause, which represents the spirit of civilization.

引例 Citations：

◎师必有名。(《礼记·檀弓下》)

(出兵必须有正当理由。)

A military campaign must have a moral justification. (*The Book of Rites*)

◎顺德者昌，逆德者亡。兵出无名，事故不成。(《汉书·高帝纪上》)

(顺应道德就会昌盛，违背道德就会灭亡。出兵没有正当名义，事情所以不会成功。)

Those who have virtue thrive; those who go against virtue perish. If a war is waged without moral justification, it will not succeed. (*The History of the Han Dynasty*)

◎庶几义声昭彰，理直气壮，师出有名，大功可就矣。(朱鼎《玉镜台记·闻鸡起舞》)

(希望正义的声音广为传扬，理由正大而气势雄壮，出兵有正当的名义，这样才可建成大功业。)

I hope the voice of justice will be heard everywhere. Be bold and confident when fighting a just war. When a military campaign has a moral justification, great victory can be achieved. (Zhu Ding: *A Tale of a Jade Dressing Table*)

shīshǐ 诗史

Historical Poetry

指诗歌的内容能够真实反映某一历史时期广阔的社会现实和重大的历史事件而具有"史"的价值。《诗经》有些诗篇反映当时历史,孔子(前551—前479)据此提出《诗经》"可以观",即包含了对《诗经》以诗征史的肯定,汉代学者很看重诗歌承载历史的功能。后来的诗论家大都强调优秀诗歌须将审美与反映现实结合起来,从而彰显诗歌的审美与认识、教育功能的统一。唐代诗人杜甫(712—770)的诗歌被称作"诗史",就是因为他的诗能够反映"安史之乱"时的真实社会,体现出深刻的忧国忧民之情。

This term refers to poetry that reflects social realities and major events of a historical period, thus possessing historical value. Some of the poems in *The Book of Songs* were about the realities of its time, which prompted Confucius (551-479 BC) to exclaim that "*The Book of Songs* enables one to understand society." This means that he viewed *The Book of Songs* as using poetry to reflect history. Han-dynasty scholars stressed the importance of poetry as a means of recording history. Subsequently, Chinese scholars of poetry believed that poetry should reflect reality through aesthetic means so as to provide aesthetic enjoyment, understanding as well as education. The poems of Tang poet Du Fu (712-770) are called "historical poetry" because they reflected what the country went through during the An Lushan-Shi Siming Rebellion and the author's acute sense of sadness about the misery the country and its people suffered in times of national crisis.

引例 Citations：

◎杜逢禄山之难，流离陇蜀，毕陈于诗，推见至隐，殆无遗事，故当时号为"诗史"。（孟棨（qǐ）《本事诗·高逸》）
（杜甫遭逢安禄山叛乱引发的灾难，先后漂泊甘肃、四川一带，所经历的一切，全都写在诗中，后人由此推知当时的很多隐约细节，几乎没有什么遗漏，所以当时人称他的诗为"诗史"。）

Du Fu fled to the provinces of Gansu and Sichuan to escape turbulences caused by the An Lushan-Shi Siming Rebellion and wrote about his experiences in poems. As his poems gave vivid and detailed accounts about events of the time, they became known as "historical poetry." (Meng Qi: *The Story of Poetry*)

◎昔人评杜诗为"诗史"，盖其以咏歌之辞，寓纪载之实，而抑扬褒贬之意，粲然于其中，虽谓之"史"可也。（文天祥《集杜诗自序》）
（过去的人评价杜甫诗为"诗史"，大概是因为他能够以诗歌形式记载真实的事件，同时批评讥刺与表扬赞美的意旨显然蕴含其中，所以称他的诗为"史"完全合适。）

People regarded the poems of Du Fu as historical poetry mostly because they described what really happened in his age, and they contained criticisms or praises of historical events. So his poems were aptly called "historical poetry." (Wen Tianxiang: Preface to *The Selected Poems of Du Fu*)

shī zhōng yǒu huà, huà zhōng yǒu shī 诗中有画，画中有诗

Painting in Poetry, Poetry in Painting

诗中有画意，画中有诗情。指诗歌与绘画作品所呈现出的审美意境融合相通的美学效果。语出苏轼（1037—1101）《书摩诘〈蓝田烟雨图〉》。绘画是造型艺术，通过众多物象构成画面给人以审美感受；诗歌是语言艺术，通过文字营造意境给人以审美感受。前者是"无声有形"的艺术，后者是"有声无形"的艺术。这一术语旨在提倡"诗歌"与"绘画"的相互渗透与融合，进而创造出天然清新、具有"诗情画意"的审美境界。苏轼这一思想对后世文学与绘画艺术的发展有着深远的影响。

This expression highlights the connection between poetry and painting in their ability to create aesthetic imagery. This idea was first put forward by Su Shi (1037-1101) in his "Notes to Wang Wei's Painting 'Mist and Rain over Lantian.'" Painting creates an aesthetic effect through images presented. Poetry, on the other hand, is a language art, which creates an aesthetic effect through the use of words. The former is an art that has shape but no sound, while the latter is an art that has sound but no shape. The term means that good poetry and painting should be fused so that a spontaneous and novel aesthetic realm can be created by a "picturesque poem" or a "poetic picture." This idea of Su Shi's had a far-reaching influence on the subsequent development of literature and painting in China.

引例 Citations：

◎味摩诘之诗，诗中有画；观摩诘之画，画中有诗。（苏轼《东坡题跋·书

摩诘〈蓝田烟雨图〉》）

（品味王维的诗，诗中有画的意境；观看王维的画，画中有诗的情感。）

When reading Wang Wei's poems, one can conjure up a picturesque image. When viewing Wang Wei's paintings, one can experience a poetic sentiment. (Su Shi: *A Collection of Su Dongpo's Prefaces and Postscripts*)

◎诗中画，性情中来者也，则画不是可拟张拟李而后作诗；画中诗，乃境趣时生者也，则诗不是便生吞生剥而后成画。真识相触，如镜写影，初何容心？今人不免唐突诗画矣。（石涛《大涤子题画诗跋》卷一"跋画"）

（所谓诗中有画，源自诗人的本真性情，故而诗中的画不是随便描摹哪个姓张姓李的人的画便能写出诗来；所谓画中有诗，乃是由当时特定的意境、情趣生发出来的，故而画中的诗不是生搬硬套某一首诗便能画成画。内心的识见与自然碰撞相融，如同镜子显现物象那么逼真，起初哪里是有意于此，今天的人[不懂得这一点]所以免不了要胡乱冒犯诗画了。）

Painting in poetry is a natural creation deriving from a poet's true aspiration; such poems cannot be composed by imitating others' paintings. Poetry in painting is inspired by a specific scene or sentiment at a given time, so it is not possible to artificially insert a poem into a painting. The way that a mind interacts with nature is as direct and unaffected as a life-like image reflected in a mirror. The effect is not deliberately intended at first. Nowadays, people do not understand this point. No wonder poetry and painting have become abused. (Shi Tao: *Dadizi's Comments on His Own Poems Inscribed on Paintings*)

shíshì-qiúshì 实事求是

Seek Truth from Facts

根据事物实际情况，正确地对待和处理问题。本指古人治学时注重事实，以求得出正确的见解或结论。后多指依据实际情况进行思考或表达，如实、正确地对待和处理问题。它既是一种关于思维或认识的方法论原则，也是一种做人的基本态度或伦理操守。其基本理念是求真、务实或诚实。

This term means handling things correctly according to realities of the situation. The term was originally used to describe the rigorous attitude of ancient Chinese scholars who paid great attention to acquiring solid facts in order to arrive at the correct understanding or conclusion. Later, it has come to mean expressing ideas or handling matters according to reality. It is a methodological principle on cognition and a fundamental principle underpinning behaviors and ethics. Basically, it calls for behaving in a practical, realistic, and honest way.

引例 Citation：

◎河间献王德……修学好古，实事求是。(《汉书·景十三王传·河间献王德》)

(河间献王刘德……喜欢学习和古代事物，在充分掌握事实的基础上求得正确的见解。)

Liu De, Prince Xian of Hejian… loved to study history and always sought the right understanding based on thorough grasp of evidence. (*The History of the Han Dynasty*)

sī 思

Reflecting / Thinking

　　心所具有的思考与辨别的能力。儒家认为"思"是人心所独有的重要功能。心能"思",因此可以不像耳目之官一样被外物牵引或遮蔽。人只有通过心之"思",才能发现内在于心的道德品性的根基,并由此通达于"天道",从而确立人之所以为人的本质。如果缺少"思"的工夫,人将丧失其主体性与独立性。

The term means the ability to reflect and evaluate. Confucian scholars considered this a unique quality of the human mind. By reflecting, a person will keep himself from being led astray or getting confused by what he sees or hears. Through reflecting, a person will discover the foundation of morality. This leads to understanding the way of heaven, and eventually, the essence of being human. Without reflecting, humans will lose their individual consciousness and independence.

引例 Citations：

◎学而不思则罔,思而不学则殆。(《论语·为政》)
(只"学"而不"思",则会迷茫昏乱;只"思"而不"学",则会疑惑危殆。)

Learning without reflecting leads to confusion; reflecting without learning leads to danger. (*The Analects*)

◎耳目之官不思,而蔽于物,物交物则引之而已矣。心之官则思。思则得之,不思则不得也。此天之所与我者,先立乎其大者,则其小者不能夺也。(《孟子·告子上》)

（耳目等器官不能思考，因而被外物的表象遮蔽。耳目与外物相接触，就会被其引向歧途。"心"这一器官能够思考，思考便能有所得，不思考便无所得。这是天赋予我的，先确立心作为大者的官能，如此则不会被耳目之官的欲望遮蔽。）

The sensory organs like ears and eyes cannot think. Therefore, they tend to be overwhelmed by the representation of external objects, and be led astray by those objects when coming into contact with them. The heart, however, is an organ capable of thinking. Thinking yields insight, while lack of it will get one nowhere. This is the gift Heaven bestows on us. One should first establish the primacy of the heart, and then eyes and ears will not be misled. (*Mencius*)

sīwén 斯文

Be Cultured and Refined

即"文"或"人文"，包括礼乐教化、典章制度等，也即诗书、礼乐、法度等精神文明的创造以及与之相关的既有差等又有调和的社会秩序。"斯"，此，这个。后"斯文"连用，也用于指读书人或文人；又衍生出文雅之意，形容一种教养或风度。

Literally, the term means "this culture." It encompasses the cultural and ethical progress created by rites, music, education, codes, and systems as well as a social order which is hierarchical but harmonious. Later, this term came to refer to the literati and extended to mean being cultured and refined.

引例 Citation：

◎天之将丧斯文也，后死者不得与于斯文也。(《论语·子罕》)

(上天如果要消灭周代的礼乐制度，那我也不可能掌握它了。)

If Heaven wished that this culture should perish, then I could do nothing about it. (*The Analects*)

sìduān 四端

Four Initiators

　　仁、义、礼、智四德的端始、萌芽。孟子(前372？—前289)认为仁、义、礼、智根于心。恻隐之心是仁之端，羞恶之心是义之端，辞让之心是礼之端，是非之心是智之端。"四端"是每一个人天生所具有的，是人之所以为人的本质特征。人只要充分扩充、发挥自己内心所固有的善端，就能够成就仁、义、礼、智四德，从而成为君子乃至圣人。

The four initiators are buds of four virtues: *ren* (仁), *yi* (义), *li* (礼), and *zhi* (智), or roughly benevolence, righteousness, propriety, and wisdom, which Mencius (372?-289 BC) believed were all rooted in man's mind. Commiseration is the initiator of benevolence. Shame is the initiator of righteousness. Deference is the initiator of propriety and a sense of right and wrong is the initiator of wisdom. The four initiators are naturally possessed by man. They are fundamental features defining a human being. Man should fully cultivate and develop his inherent kindness, then he can accomplish the four virtues, and consequently become a man of virtue or even a sage.

引例 Citation：

◎ 凡有四端于我者，知皆扩而充之矣，若火之始然，泉之始达。苟能充之，足以保四海；苟不充之，不足以事父母。(《孟子·公孙丑上》)

（凡是具有"四端"的人，知道把它们扩充起来，就好像火刚开始燃烧，泉水刚开始涌出。如果能够扩充"四端"，就足以安定天下；如果不能扩充"四端"，都不足以奉养父母。）

All who have the four initiators in them should know how to cultivate them, so that these initiators will grow, just like a fire that has started burning, or a spring that has started gushing out. If people can cultivate and expand the four initiators, they can bring stability to the world. Otherwise, they can hardly provide for their parents. (*Mencius*)

sìhǎi 四海

Four Seas

全国各地或世界各地。古人认为中国的疆域四面环海，各依方位称"东海""南海""西海"和"北海"，合称"四海"。它蕴含着远古中国人关于中国和世界的地理图景："九州"居"天下"之中，"天下"由"九州"及其周边"四海"组成，中国是"海内"，外国则是"海外"。在古人那里，"四海"大多统指天下，并不确指某个海域，有时用来指陆地四周的海，有时又指"四海"所环绕的陆地。

Four Seas refer to the territory of China or the entire world. The ancient Chinese believed that China was a land surrounded by Four Seas – the East, West, North, and South seas. The term suggests what the ancient Chinese conceived to be the map of China and the world: Nine *zhou* (regions) were located at the center of *tianxia* (all under heaven). *Tianxia* consisted of nine *zhou* and its surrounding Four Seas. China was within the Four Seas, while foreign lands were outside the Four Seas. In ancient China, Four Seas referred to all under heaven in most cases, and did not denote a specific body of water. Therefore, the term was used sometimes to mean the seas surrounding the land, and sometimes to specify the land surrounded by the Four Seas.

引例 Citation：

◎君子敬而无失，与人恭而有礼，四海之内皆兄弟也。(《论语・颜渊》)
（君子做事认真而不出差错，待人谦恭而合于礼，那么天下所有的人都是他的兄弟。）

A man of virtue always does things conscientiously without making any mistakes and treats people respectfully and appropriately. Then all within the Four Seas will be his brothers. (*The Analects*)

sìshū 四书

Four Books

　　《论语》《孟子》《大学》《中庸》等四部儒家经典的合称。《大学》《中庸》原是《礼记》中的两篇，在唐代以前，并没有引起人们的特别重视。随着唐宋以来儒学的复兴，《大学》《中庸》经过唐代韩愈（768—824）、李翱（772—836）的表彰，宋代程颢（1032—1085）、程颐（1033—1107）兄弟和朱熹（1130—1200）的推崇，被赋予了新的意义，其地位逐渐提升，与《论语》《孟子》并列，合称"四书"。朱熹所著《四书章句集注》确立了"四书"的经典地位。"四书"成为了宋明理学家创建、阐发自身思想的重要素材，对后世儒学的发展产生了深远影响。

This term refers collectively to the four Confucian classics: *The Analects, Mencius, The Great Learning,* and *The Doctrine of the Mean. The Great Learning* and *The Doctrine of the Mean* originally were two sections of *The Book of Rites,* but before the Tang Dynasty they did not attract much attention. Following the revival of Confucianism which began in the Tang and Song dynasties, through the advocacy of Han Yu (768-824) and Li Ao (772-836) of the Tang Dynasty, Cheng Hao (1032-1085), Cheng Yi (1033-1107) and Zhu Xi (1130-1200) of the Song Dynasty, *The Great Learning* and *The Doctrine of the Mean* were given new meaning. Their standing was gradually elevated, and they were regarded just as important as *The Analects* and *Mencius*. The four were then collectively known as the Four Books. *Commentaries on the Four Books,* written by Zhu Xi, established the dominant position of the Four Books, which formed the foundation for the neo-Confucian scholars of the Song and Ming dynasties. The Four Books became the source from which the neo-Confucian scholars drew inspiration to further their learning, and thus exerted a profound influence on the development of Confucianism.

引例 Citation：

◎如《大学》《中庸》《语》《孟》四书，道理粲然。(《朱子语类》卷十四)
(如《大学》《中庸》《论语》《孟子》四部经典，其中的道理明白易懂。)

The principles in the Four Books, i.e., *The Great Learning, The Doctrine of the Mean, The Analects,* and *Mencius,* are illuminating and easy to follow. (*Classified Conversations of Master Zhu Xi*)

体

Ti

"体"作为文艺学、美学范畴，主要含义有三：其一，指文学艺术的某一门类、流派、体式、作品区别于其他文学艺术门类、流派、体式、作品的整体特征。它是包含了文学艺术的体式、内容、语言、风格等诸要素在内所呈现出的总体形态与艺术特征。其二，指文学艺术作品的风格，不包括体式、形式等方面的内容。其三，指文学作品的基本样式，即文体或文学体制。历代文论家对文体的分类不尽相同，比如南朝梁昭明太子萧统（501—531）《文选》将文体分为38种。中国古代文学的文体丰富多样，各有自己的基本样式与写作要求，而风格即是作者的艺术个性在作品中的显现，有时也表现为一个时代、一个流派的文学特征。这一术语经常与人名、朝代名等结合，如骚体、陶体、建安体等，用来指称与作品风格相关的艺术特征并广泛运用于文艺批评与鉴赏中。

Ti (体) has three different meanings in the study of literature, art, and aesthetics. First, it refers to features that distinguish one particular category, form, or literary school from others. These features represent the overall form and artistic characteristics, including the structure, content, language, style, and other essential elements. Second, it refers only to literary and artistic style, not their form or shape. Third, it refers to the basic literary and artistic form, i.e., the writing style and literary genre. Scholars of literary theory in different historical periods did not use the same standards to classify literary styles. For example, Xiao Tong (501-531, Crown Prince Zhaoming of the Liang Dynasty during the Southern Dynasties) classified literary and artistic works into 38 styles or categories in his *Selections of Refined Literature.* There is a wide range of writing styles and literary genres in classical Chinese literature, each with its own style and writing requirements. The style of a literary work reflects the author's individual artistic temperament, and, sometimes, also the literary and artistic trend in a particular era. This term is often used together with the name of a person or a dynasty to describe literary and artistic features peculiar to a school of literature. Examples are the Sao Style (represented by the famous poem, *Li Sao*, written by renowned poet Qu Yuan), Tao Style (represented by poet Tao Yuanming), and Jian'an Style (named after the period of Jian'an during the Han Dynasty). The term is widely used in literary criticism and appreciation.

引例 Citations：

◎夫人善于自见，而文非一体，鲜能备善，是以各以所长，相轻所短。（曹丕《典论·论文》）

（人总是善于看到自己的优点，然而文章不止一种文体，很少有人擅长所有文体，因此各人总是以自己所擅长的文体写作而轻视别人所不擅长的文体。）

People are always quick to see their own strengths. However, given the rich variety of literary styles, few people are accomplished in all of them. Therefore, people always write in the styles they are good at while taking lightly other people's works written in styles they happen to be weak in. (Cao Pi: On Literary Classics)

◎自汉至魏，四百余年，辞人才子，文体三变。（《宋书·谢灵运传论》）

（自汉至魏，四百多年，写诗文的才子 [众多]，而诗文的体制风格,也经历了三次大的变化。）

For more than 400 years from the Han Dynasty to the Wei Dynasty, numerous talented poets came to the fore, and the styles of poetry and essay writing went through three major transformations. (*The History of Song of the Southern Dynasties*)

tiānrén-héyī 天人合一

Heaven and Man Are United as One.

　　一种认为天地人相通的世界观和思维方式。这种世界观旨在强调天地和人之间的整体性和内在联系，突出了天对于人或人事的根源性意义，表现了人在与天的联系中寻求生命、秩序与价值基础的努力。"天人合一"在历史上有不同的表现方式，如天人同类、同气或者同理等。如孟子（前372？—前289）认为通过心的反思可以知性、知天，强调心、性和天之间的统一。宋儒寻求天理、人性和人心之间的相通。老子则主张"人法地，地法天，天法道"。根据对天和人理解的不同，"天人合一"也会具有不同的意义。

The term represents a world outlook and a way of thinking which hold that heaven and earth and man are interconnected. This world outlook emphasizes the integration and inherent relationship between heaven, earth, and man. It highlights the fundamental significance of nature to man or human affairs, and describes the endeavor made by man to pursue life, order, and values through interaction with nature. The term has different ways of expression in history, such as heaven and man are of the same category, sharing the same vital energy, or sharing the same principles. Mencius (372?-289 BC), for one, believed that through mental reflection one could gain understanding of human nature and heaven, emphasizing the unity of mind, human nature, and heaven. Confucian scholars of the Song Dynasty sought to connect the principles of heaven, human nature, and the human mind. Laozi maintained that "man's law is earthly, earth's law is natural, and heaven's law is Dao." Depending on a different understanding of heaven and man, the term may have different meanings.

引例 Citations：

◎以类合之，天人一也。(董仲舒《春秋繁露·阴阳义》)
(以事类相合来看，天与人是一体的。)

In terms of integration of categories, heaven and man are one. (Dong Zhongshu: *Luxuriant Gems of The Spring and Autumn Annals*)

◎儒者则因明致诚，因诚致明，故天人合一，致学而可以成圣，得天而未始遗人。(张载《正蒙·乾称》)
(儒者则由明察人伦而通达天理之诚，由通达天理之诚而洞明世事，因此天与人相合为一，通过学习而可以成为圣人，把握天理而不曾遗失对人伦的洞察。)

A Confucian scholar is sincere because of his understanding, and he achieves understanding because of his sincerity. That is why heaven and man are united as one. One can become a sage through studies, and master heaven's law without losing understanding of man's law. (Zhang Zai: *Enlightenment Through Confucian Teachings*)

tiānrénzhīfēn 天人之分

Distinction Between Man and Heaven

一种认为天与人相分别的世界观和思维方式。此说最初由荀子（前

313？—前238）所提出，他反对将人世的道德、秩序的来源或依据寄托于天。荀子认为，天与人各有其职分，不应混淆。天地日月的运行、寒暑水旱的出现，都属于天职的领域，有其常道，与人事无关，也非人力所及。而人的道德、人世的治乱则属于人职的范围，人应对道德的养成及社会的治理负责。只有明确了"天人之分"，人才能在天所赋予和确立的基础之上发挥人的能力而不是僭越到人无法用力的领域。

This term refers to a world outlook and a way of thinking which hold that heaven and man are different. This explanation was first put forward by Xunzi (313?-238 BC), who did not believe that human morality and the order of human society emanated from heaven. He argued that heaven and man each had a different role and that they should not be mixed. Temporal changes of heaven and earth as well as the occurrence of seasonal changes in temperature and rainfall all belonged to the domain of heaven. They had their normal path, unrelated to human affairs, and were beyond the reach of human power. On the other hand, man's morality and order in the world belonged to the realm of man. People should be responsible for moral development and social order. Only by making a clear distinction between heaven and man could one develop his abilities on the basis established by heaven, without overstepping into a domain where man was unable to exert his power.

引例 Citation：

◎天行有常，不为尧存，不为桀亡。……强本而节用，则天不能贫；养备而动时，则天不能病；修道而不贰，则天不能祸。……故明于天人之分，则可谓至人矣。(《荀子·天论》)
（天的运行有其常道，不因为尧在位而存在，不因为桀在位而消失。……加强农事而节省用度，则天不能使之贫乏；供养充足而活动适时，则天不能使之疾病；循行正道而坚定不移，则天不能加以灾祸。……因此能够明晓天与人的区分，就可以称之为最高明的人了。）

Nature's ways are constant. They did not exist because Yao was on the throne or disappear because Jie was the ruler... When you work diligently in agriculture and are frugal in expenditures, nature cannot impoverish you. When you are well provided for with what you need and work at the proper time, nature cannot make you sick. When you firmly follow the right path, nature cannot bring you disaster... Therefore, he who understands the distinction between nature and man may be called the wisest man. (*Xunzi*)

tiānzǐ 天子

Son of Heaven

"天"之子，指帝王、君主，即帝国或王朝的最高统治者。古人认为，帝王、君主秉上天旨意统治天下，其权力乃天所授，故称帝王、君主为天子。这个名称肯定了帝王、君主的权力来自上天所赐的正当性和神圣性，同时也对之构成一定的约束。这和西方的"君权神授"的观念相似，但有根本不同：中国的"天"不同于西方的"神"，而且蕴含着"天人感应"的思想，即"天"的旨意与人心、民意相贯通。

The Son of Heaven refers to the emperor or monarch, the supreme ruler of an empire or dynasty. People in ancient times believed that a monarch ruled the world by Heaven's decree and with its mandate, hence he was called the Son of Heaven. This term asserted that a ruler's authority was legitimate and sacred, as it was bestowed by Heaven, but to some extent, it also restricted the exercise of this power. This has some similarity to the Western concept of the divine right of kings by the grace of God, but there are fundamental differences. *Tian* (天), the Chinese word for Heaven, is not the same as the Western term "God." Rather, the Chinese term also implies the idea of interaction between Heaven and man, which means that the decree of Heaven also embodies popular will and popular support.

引例 Citations：

◎明明天子，令闻不已。(《诗经·大雅·江汉》)

（勤勤勉勉的周天子，美好的声誉流传不息。）

So diligent is the Son of Heaven! His fame will forever be remembered. (*The Book of Songs*)

◎德侔天地者称皇帝，天祐而子之，号称天子。(董仲舒《春秋繁露·三代改制质文》)

（道德可与天地齐等的人做皇帝，上天保佑他，以他为子，所以号称"天子"。）

A man whose virtue is equal to that of heaven and earth can be an emperor. Heaven blesses him and takes him as his son, so he is called the Son of Heaven. (Dong Zhongshu: *Luxuriant Gems of The Spring and Autumn Annals*)

wēnróu-dūnhòu 温柔敦厚

Mild, Gentle, Sincere, and Broad-minded

指儒家经典《诗经》所具有的温和宽厚的精神及教化作用。秦汉时期的儒学认为，《诗经》虽然有讽刺、劝谏的内容，但是重在疏导，不直言斥责，大多数诗篇情理中和，在潜移默化中使读者受到感化，养成敦实忠厚的德性，从而达到以诗教化的目的。温柔敦厚的诗教观是儒家中庸之道的体现，以中正、平和为审美标准，这也成为对于文艺创作风格的要求，体现为以含蓄为美、以教化为重。

This term refers to the mild and broad-minded manner with which the Confucian classic, *The Book of Songs,* edifies people. Confucian scholars during the Qin and Han dynasties believed that although some poems of *The Book of Songs* were satirical and remonstrative in tone, it still focused on persuading people instead of just reproving them. Most of the poems in the book were moderate in tone and meant to encourage the reader to learn to be moderate and honest. Encouraging people to be mild and gentle, sincere and broad-minded is a manifestation of Confucian doctrine of the mean, and being fair and gentle is an aesthetic value, which is also a standard for literary and artistic style that stresses the need for being gentle in persuasion and for edification.

引例 Citations：

◎入其国，其教可知也。其为人也，温柔敦厚，《诗》教也。(《礼记·经解》)

(进入一个国家，能看出国民的教养。民众的为人如果温柔敦厚，那就是《诗经》的教化之功。)

When you enter a state, you can find out whether its people are proper in behavior. If they show themselves to be mild and gentle, sincere and broad-minded, they must have learned it from *The Book of Songs*. (*The Book of Rites*)

◎温柔敦厚，诗教之本也。有温柔敦厚之性情，乃能有温柔敦厚之诗。(朱庭珍《筱(xiǎo)园诗话》卷三)

(温柔敦厚，是诗歌教化的根本。只有具备温柔敦厚的性情，才能写出温柔敦厚的诗歌。)

Teaching people to be mild and gentle, sincere and broad-minded is the basic purpose of poetry education. One can write poetry with such characteristics only if one is endowed with such good qualities. (Zhu Tingzhen: *Xiaoyuan's Comments on Poetry*)

wénbǐ 文笔

Writing and Writing Technique

泛指各类文章。经历了不同时期的概念变化，两汉时泛指文章的技法、风格及各类文章。魏晋南北朝时期，文论家们认识到不同文体的特性，首先将文笔与经典解释类著作相区分，用"文""笔"分别指纯文学写作和应用文写作；继之又以外部形式作为区分标准，将诗赋颂赞等文学类作品与奏章书策等"杂笔"进行区分，提出有韵为文、无韵为笔的观点。梁元帝萧绎 (508—554) 以内容为尺度，进一步提出"文"（诗赋等）不仅有韵，还应该表达内心的情感并有华丽的辞藻；而"笔"（应用文）只需要一般写作能力即可。今"文笔"主要指文章的技法与语言风格。

The term generally refers to different types of writings. Its meanings have evolved over time. During the Western and Eastern Han dynasties, it generally referred to writing techniques, writing styles, and various types of articles. During the Wei, Jin, and the Southern and Northern dynasties, literary scholars began to identify different features in different types of writings. They distinguished, for the first time, literary writings from those interpreting classical works, and identified pure literature as literary writings and practical writings as technical writings. They subsequently distinguished, on the basis of form, literary works such as poems, *fu* (赋 descriptive prose interspersed with verse), *song* (颂 essays of extolment), and *zan* (赞 essay of commendation) from essays such as memorials, documents, and policy proposals submitted to the emperor by officials. They concluded that all writings with rhyme were literary writings and those without were technical writings. Xiao Yi (508-554), Emperor Yuan of the Liang Dynasty, argued further that literary writings should not only have rhyme, but also express the author's inner feelings and use elaborate rhetoric, while technical writings required only general writing skills. Today, this term mainly refers to writing techniques and language styles.

引例 Citations：

◎无韵者笔也，有韵者文也。(刘勰《文心雕龙·总术》)
(没有固定节奏和韵律的作品称为"笔"，有固定节奏和韵律的作品称为"文"。)

Writings without rhyme or rhythm are technical writings while those with rhyme and rhythm are literary ones. (Liu Xie: *The Literary Mind and the Carving of Dragons*)

◎少有志气，博学洽闻，以文笔著称。(《晋书·习凿齿传》)
([习凿齿]少年时有志气，博学多闻，以写文章著称。)

Ambitious and studious from a young age, Xi Zaochi was an erudite scholar known for his writings and writing techniques. (*The History of the Jin Dynasty*)

wénxué 文学

Literature / Scholars / Education Officials

原义为博通前代文献,"文"指文献,"学"是关于文献的学问。后泛指文章、文献以及关于文章、文献的各种知识与学问。主要含义有三:其一,先秦两汉时期,指关于古代文献特别是诗书礼乐、典章制度等人文方面的知识与学问。魏晋南北朝以后,"文学"一词大体与今天的文学概念接近,但包含人文学术的内容。近代以来,西方的文学观念传入中国,"文学"一词逐步演变指用语言创造审美形象的一门艺术,但传统意义上的"文学"范畴仍为章太炎(1869—1936)等少数学者沿用。这一术语的最初含义决定中国现当代主流的文学观念仍坚持从大文化的意义上看待文学现象,强调文学的审美价值与人文学术的内在联系,而与西方的"文学"术语强调文学之独立审美价值有所区别。其二,泛指古代各类文章及文献。其三,指以著书立说、教学等方式传播学问的文人与掌管文教的官员。

Originally, the term meant to command a good knowledge of documents from pervious dynasties. *Wen* (文) referred to documents, and *xue* (学) referred to the study of these documents. Later, the term referred to articles and documents in general as well as the knowledge about those documentations. The term had three main meanings. Firstly, from the pre-Qin period to the end of the Eastern Han Dynasty, it meant knowledge of ancient literature, especially that of humanities including poetry, history, rites and music, as well as works of laws and regulations. Starting from the Wei and Jin dynasties, the term basically became equivalent to today's concept of literature, but it also referred to academic writings on humanities. With the introduction of the Western concept of literature in recent history, the term gradually evolved to mean a pursuit that uses language to create aesthetic images. However, a few scholars, such as Zhang Taiyan (1869-1936), stuck to its traditional definition. The original meaning of the term determined the mainstream view on literature in contemporary China, which focuses on examining a literary phenomenon in the broader cultural context and emphasizing the intrinsic relationship between the aesthetic values of literature and liberal arts. This is somewhat different from the Western notion of literature which highlights the independent nature of literary appreciation. Secondly, the term refers broadly to various kinds of articles and documents in ancient times. Thirdly, it refers to scholars who promote learning through writing and teaching, as well as officials in charge of culture and education.

引例 Citations：

◎文学：子游、子夏。(《论语·先进》)

([弟子中]博学与熟悉古代文献的，是子游和子夏。)

Among the disciples of Confucius, Ziyou and Zixia have a good knowledge of ancient literature. (*The Analects*)

◎于是汉兴，萧何次律令，韩信申军法，张苍为章程，叔孙通定礼仪，则文学彬彬稍进，《诗》《书》往往间（jiàn）出矣。(《史记·太史公自序》)

(这时汉朝兴起，萧何编订法令，韩信申明军法，张苍订立历数和度量衡标准，叔孙通确定礼仪，而后文章与学问出众的人才逐渐进入朝廷，失传的《诗经》《尚书》等典籍也不断被发现。)

At that time, the Han Dynasty was on the rise, with Xiao He codifying laws, Han Xin promulgating military rules, Zhang Cang formulating the calendar and measurements, and Shusun Tong establishing ceremonial rites. Soon, literary talent who excelled in writing and learning took up positions in the imperial court. Lost classics such as *The Book of Songs* and *The Book of History* were rediscovered one after another. (*Records of the Historian*)

◎大抵儒学本《礼》，荀子是也；史学本《书》与《春秋》，马迁是也；玄学本《易》，庄子是也；文学本《诗》，屈原是也。（刘熙载《艺概·文概》）
（大致来说，儒学以《礼》为依据，荀子即是这样；史学以《尚书》和《春秋》为典范，司马迁即是这样；玄学以《周易》为根基，庄子即是这样；文学以《诗经》为本源，屈原即是这样。）

Generally speaking, Confucian studies are based on *The Book of Rites*, as exemplified by Xunzi. Historiography is modeled on *The Book of History* and *The Spring and Autumn Annals,* as exemplified by Sima Qian. Metaphysical studies are based on *The Book of Changes*, as exemplified by Zhuangzi. Literature has its root in *The Book of Songs*, as exemplified by Qu Yuan. (Liu Xizai: *Overview of Literary Theories*)

wénzhāng 文章

Literary Writing

泛指一切著述，包括今天意义上的文章和著作。先秦时这一术语包含在文学之内，两汉时"文章"一词与"文学"对举，指一切用文字写下来的文辞、篇章、史书、论著，六朝时"文章"与"文学"并列，开始指后世所说的审美范畴的"文学"，但仍作为统括一切文体的范畴使用。"章"意为一曲音乐演奏完毕，或一首完整的音乐，故此术语强调作品意义和结构的完整，注重文章写作手法与技巧；"文"和"章"都有花纹、色彩错杂的意思，"文章"相当于美的形式，故此术语隐含了审美观念。早期"文章"的概念与"文学"概念有一定联系又有所区别。"文章"偏重于辞章美文，说明了人们对于文章审美价值的逐渐重视。

The term refers to all kinds of writings, including what we call essays and books today. In the Pre-Qin period, this term was subsumed under literature. During the Han Dynasty, the term referred to writings other than *wenxue* (文学 documents of previous dynasties) to specifically mean essays, articles, history books, and treatises. In the Six Dynasties, the term, together with *wenxue*, began to assume the meaning of what later generations meant by literature, that is, writings for aesthetic appreciation which encompass every type of literary works. *Zhang* (章) also implies a movement of music played to its finish, or a single piece of music. Therefore, the term focuses on both meaning and structure as well as writing skills and techniques. Both Chinese characters in the term have the meaning of interwoven patterns and colors. Together, they signify a beautiful form, giving the term an aesthetic connotation. The earlier concept of the term is related to but different from that of *wenxue*, with the former focusing more on elegant diction and style, indicating increasing attention to the aesthetic value of literary works.

引例 Citations：

◎文章者，盖情性之风标，神明之律吕也。蕴思含毫，游心内运，放言落纸，气韵天成。(《南齐书·文学传论》)

（所谓文章，乃是人的感情性格变化的风向标、内在精神的一种量器。下笔之前蓄积文思，内心思绪自由驰骋，等到形诸纸墨时，文章的气韵自然天成。）

Literary writings reflect one's moods and disposition, or give expression to one's inner world. Before writing, one should gather his thoughts and free his mind so as to transcend the limitations of time and space. Thus, once he starts writing, his work will achieve its flavor naturally. (*The History of Qi of the Southern Dynasties*)

◎圣贤书辞，总称"文章"，非采而何？（刘勰《文心雕龙·情采》）

（古代圣贤的著作文辞，都叫做"文章"，这不是因为它们都具有文采吗？）

Writings by sages in ancient times are all called "literary writings." Isn't this because they all have literary elegance? (Liu Xie: *The Literary Mind and the Carving of Dragons*)

Wú-Yuè-tóngzhōu 吴越同舟

/Wú-Yuè-tóngzhōu/

People of Wu and Yue Are in the Same Boat.

吴、越两国人同乘一条船。比喻双方虽有旧怨，但面临共同的危难困境，也会团结一致，相互救助。春秋时代，吴、越是相互仇视的邻国，但当两国人同船渡江，遭遇风浪时，他们却相互救援，如同一个人的左右手一样。它包含的思想是：敌友不是绝对的，也不是永恒的，在一定的境遇下可以化敌为友。

In the Spring and Autumn Period, Wu and Yue were neighboring states which were hostile to each other. Wu and Yue people being in the same boat is a metaphor for overcoming old grievances to face common danger. When people from these two states were crossing a river in the same boat and encountered a storm, they had to work together to save themselves; in that sense, they were just like the left and right hands of the same person. The story implies that there is no absolute and perpetual enmity or friendship. Under certain circumstances, an enemy can be turned into a friend.

引例 Citation：

◎吴越之人，同舟济江，中流遇风波，其相救如左右手者，所患同也。(《孔丛子·论势》)

(吴、越两国的人同乘一条船渡江，中途遭遇风浪，他们之所以像一个人的左右手一样相互救援，是因为他们遇到共同的危难。)

People of the states of Wu and Yue were crossing a river in the same boat when they encountered strong winds and waves midstream. To save themselves from a common peril, they worked together like the left and right hands of the same person. (*Collected Works of the Confucian Family*)

wǔjīng 五经

Five Classics

《诗》《书》《礼》《易》《春秋》等五部儒家经典的合称。先秦时期有"六经"之说，指《诗》《书》《礼》《乐》《易》《春秋》，因《乐》已亡佚（一说无文字），故汉代多称"五经"。从汉武帝（前156—前87）立"五经博士"起，"五经"之学成为中国学术、文化和思想的根本。从内容上来说，"五经"各有所偏重，如《诗》言志、《书》言事等，因其不同而互补，故构成一个整体。历代儒者通过对文本的不断解释，为这些经典赋予了丰富的意义。"五经"之学包括了中国传统文化对于世界秩序与价值的根本理解，是"道"的集中体现。

The term refers to the five Confucian classics: *The Book of Songs*, *The Book of History*, *The Book of Rites*, *The Book of Changes,* and *The Spring and Autumn Annals.* In the pre-Qin period, the term "Six Classics" was used, referring to *The Book of Songs*, *The Book of History*, *The Book of Rites*, *The Book of Music*, *The Book of Changes*, and *The Spring and Autumn Annals*. *The Book of Music,* did not exist in written form, hence people often used the term "Five Classics" during the Han Dynasty. After Emperor Wu of the Han Dynasty (156-87 BC) established the title of "Academician of the Five Classics," study of these works became the foundation of Chinese learning, culture, and thought. In terms of content, the Five Classics each has its own focus; for instance, *The Book of Songs* deals with aspirations, and *The Book of History* chronicles events. Different in focus but complementing each other, they form an integral collection of classics. Throughout history, Confucian scholars added significant meaning to these classics with their interpretations of the original texts. The Five Classics comprise traditional Chinese culture's fundamental understanding of world order and values, epitomizing the concept of Dao.

引例 Citation：

◎ "五经"何谓？谓《易》《尚书》《诗》《礼》《春秋》也。(《白虎通义·五经》)

("五经"是什么？是《易》《尚书》《诗》《礼》《春秋》等五部典籍。)

Which are the Five Classics? They are: *The Book of Songs*, *The Book of History*, *The Book of Rites*, *The Book of Changes*, and *The Spring and Autumn Annals*. (*Debates of the White Tiger Hall*)

xiāoyáo 逍遥

Carefree

  人的心灵的一种自由、无待的状态。最初由庄子（前369？—前286）提出并以之名篇。庄子认为，人的心灵可以超越于形体无法逃避、无可奈何的境遇之上，消除对于物的依赖，进而达到心灵的自由、无碍。西晋郭象（？—312）重新解释了"逍遥"之义，认为有待之物能够安于各自的性分（fèn）即达到了"逍遥"。

The term refers to a state of mind totally free from all constraints. It was first proposed by Zhuangzi (369?-286 BC) in one of his most well-known essays. According to him, people's minds can go beyond predicament in a way that their bodies cannot, so mentally they can be independent of material concerns and free of all worries. Guo Xiang (?-312) of the Western Jin Dynasty had a new definition of the term: By acting in accordance with its own nature, everything can be free of troubles and worries.

引例 Citations：

◎芒然彷徨乎尘垢之外，逍遥乎无为之业。(《庄子·大宗师》)
（安闲无待地神游于尘世之外，逍遥自在于自然无为的境地。）

People should seek carefree enjoyment beyond the constraints of the human world. (*Zhuangzi*)

◎夫小大虽殊，而放于自得之场，则物任其性，事称其能，各当其分（fèn），逍遥一也。(郭象《庄子注》卷一)
（事物虽然有大小的不同，但若安放于自得的范围内，则每一事物都按照其本性发展，功用与其本性相合，担当各自的职分，则它们所达到的逍遥是一样的。）

Things, big and small, are different from each other. But when they are placed where they should be, each of them will develop as its nature dictates, shoulder their proper responsibilities, and ultimately achieve the same degree of freedom. (Guo Xiang: *Annotations on Zhuangzi*)

xiǎorén 小人

Petty Man

　　"小人"最初用以表明人的社会身份与地位，通常指被统治者或地位低下之人。后世又以人的德行高下来界定"小人"，德行卑下者被称作"小人"（与"君子"相对）。"小人"只关注和追逐个人的权力或利益，为了获取私利不惜违背道义，缺乏对"道"的理解与尊重。

The term was originally used to indicate a person's social status, usually referring to the rulers' subjects or those low in social ranking. Later generations also used the term to indicate one's moral standard in a disapproving way. Those of base character were called petty men as opposed to men of virtue. A petty man only pursues his personal interests or profits, even by violating morality and righteousness; and such people have no understanding of or regard for Dao.

引例 Citations：

◎君子喻于义，小人喻于利。(《论语·里仁》)
（君子知晓并遵循义，小人知晓并追逐利。）

A man of virtue understands and observes what is morally right; while a petty man only has his eyes on and goes after what brings him personal gains. (*The Analects*)

◎苟安务得，所以为小人。（朱熹《论语集注》卷二）

（苟且偷安务求得利，因此是小人。）

They are petty men because they only seek ease and comfort of the moment and pursue personal gains. (Zhu Xi: *The Analects Variorum*)

xíng'érshàng 形而上

What Is Above Form / The Metaphysical

无形或未成形质，一般以此指称有形事物的依据。出自《周易·系辞上》（与"形而下"相对而言）。"形"指形体，"形而上"是指在形体出现之前，也即无形者。此无形者被称为"道"。

The term means what is formless or has no formal substance yet. It generally indicates the basis of physical things. The term "what is above form" comes from *The Book of Changes* and is used as the opposite of "what is under form." "Form" indicates physical shape. "What is above form" refers to the state before a physical shape emerges, namely, formlessness. That which is formless is called "Dao."

引例 **Citation**：

◎形而上者谓之道，形而下者谓之器。（《周易·系辞上》）

（未成形质者称为"道"，已成形质者称为"器"。）

What is above form is called Dao, and what is under form is called "an object." (*The Book of Changes*)

xíng'érxià 形而下

What Is Under Form / The Physical

有形或已成形质，一般指实际存在的具体事物。出自《周易·系辞上》（与"形而上"相对而言）。"形"指形体，"形而下"指在形体出现之后，也即有形者。此有形者被称为"器"。"形而下"的存在以"形而上"为依据。

The term means what has a form or what has a formal substance. It generally indicates existing and concrete things. The term "what is under form" comes from *The Book of Changes*. It is used as the opposite of "what is above form." "Form" indicates physical shape. "What is under form" refers to the state after a physical shape has emerged, namely, physical existence. That which has a form is called "an object." What is under form takes what is above form as the basis of its existence.

引例 Citation：

◎形而上者谓之道，形而下者谓之器。(《周易·系辞上》)
（未成形质者称为"道"，已成形质者称为"器"。）

What is above form is called Dao, and what is under form is called "an object." (*The Book of Changes*)

xìngjì 兴寄

Xingji (Association and Inner Sustenance)

运用比兴、寄托等艺术手法，使诗歌情感蕴藉、内涵深厚、寄托感慨。由初唐时代的陈子昂（659—700）首次提出。"兴"是由外物触发而兴发情感，"寄"是寄托某种寓意。兴寄最初是指诗人的感兴要有寓意，达到托物言志的目的；后来引申为诗歌要有赞美或讽刺的寓意。兴寄这一术语继承了先秦时代感物起兴的诗歌传统，强调诗歌的感兴之中要有深沉的寄托，是比兴理论的重要发展，对于盛唐诗歌摆脱齐梁时代诗歌追求华彩而摒弃寄托的创作态度、推动唐诗健康发展有很大作用。

The term means the use of analogy, association, and inner sustenance in writing a poem to give implicit expression to one's sentiments, thus enabling the poem to convey a subtle message. The term was first used by the Tang-dynasty poet Chen Zi'ang (659-700). *Xing* (兴) means the development of inner feelings invoked by external objects, and *ji* (寄) means finding sustenance in them. Later it was extended to mean that poetry should be written to convey a message of praise or satire. The term carried on the pre-Qin poetical tradition of creating inspiration by writing about a subject and stressed that while depicting sentiments in poetry, the poet should find sustenance in it. The term represented an important development of the theory of analogy and association. It played a major role in ensuring that poets in the prime of the Tang Dynasty broke away from the poetic style of the Qi and Liang of the Southern Dynasties, which pursued ornate language instead of inner sustenance, thus enabling Tang poetry to develop in a healthy way.

引例 Citations:

◎仆尝暇时观齐梁间诗，彩丽竞繁而兴寄都绝。每以永叹，思古人常恐逶迤颓靡、风雅不作，以耿耿也。（陈子昂《修竹篇（并序）》）
（我曾经在闲暇时读齐梁时期的诗歌，这些诗辞藻堆砌、竞相华丽，但是兴寄的味道一点儿都没有。我常为此长叹，推想古人经常担心诗风渐至颓废华靡，《诗经》的风雅传统不再振兴，心中定会耿耿不平。）

When I read the poems of the Qi and Liang of the Southern Dynasties in my leisure time, I found them full of ornate rhetoric heaped together without sustenance. I often feel resigned as I can well imagine that the ancients were always concerned about poetry becoming decadent and the tradition of objectively reflecting reality as shown in *The Book of Songs* getting lost. (Chen Zi'ang: "The Bamboo" with a Preface)

◎仆尝病兴寄之作堙（yīn）郁于世，辞有枝叶，荡而成风，益用慨然。（柳宗元《答贡士沈起书》）
（我曾经担忧那些有兴寄特色的作品被埋没掉，文章追求浮华枝叶，恣纵成为风尚，这个时候更需要作品有感慨和意味。）

I was concerned that the works based on association and inner sustenance would get lost and that writings with only elaborate rhetoric would prevail. We really need works that have substance. (Liu Zongyuan: Letter to Scholar Shen Qi)

xìngqù 兴趣

Xingqu (Charm)

"兴"中所蕴含的趣或者是"兴"发时心物交会所产生的趣（情趣、意趣等）。是诗歌中所蕴含的、读者通过欣赏而获得的特定的审美趣味。南宋诗论家严羽（？—1264）在《沧浪诗话》中倡导诗歌的感染力，反对直接说理，主张让读者在品读和感悟中得到愉悦和满足。这一术语后来成为评价诗歌的重要标准，明清诗学也受到积极影响。

The term refers to charm inherent in an inspiration, or charm created when the object or scene depicted in a poem is appreciated. It is a type of aesthetic enjoyment contained in a poem which is gained through the reader's act of appreciation. In *Canglang's Criticism on Poetry*, Yan Yu (?-1264), a poetry critic of the Southern Song Dynasty, voiced his love for poetry's emotional charm and argued against direct expression of an idea in poetry. He stressed the need to enable readers to gain insight and satisfaction in a natural way through personal reflection and contemplation. This term later became an important criterion for evaluating poetry, exerting a strong influence on the poetry theories of the Ming and Qing dynasties.

引例 Citations：

◎诗者，吟咏情性也。盛唐诸人惟在兴趣，羚羊挂角，无迹可求。（严羽《沧浪诗话·诗辨》）

（诗歌吟咏的是本性真情。盛唐诗人的诗作特别着意兴趣，如同羚羊晚上将角挂在树上睡觉，没有任何痕迹可寻。）

One should write poetry only to express one's true sentiments and personality. In their poems, Tang-dynasty poets made particular efforts to inspire meaning, charm, and emotion. Their style is like an antelope hooking its horns onto a tree when sleeping at night, so that its trace cannot be found. (Yan Yu: *Canglang's Criticism on Poetry*)

◎古诗多在兴趣，微辞隐义，有足感人。而宋人多好以诗议论。夫以诗议论，即奚不为文而为诗哉？（屠隆《文论》）

（古代诗作多注重审美情趣的传达，用词含蓄而寓意隐微，足以感染读者。而宋代诗人大多借诗歌来论事说理。用诗歌论事说理，那为何不写成文章而非要写成诗呢？）

Classical poems mostly focused on inspiring meaning, charm, and emotion through hints with subtle wording and implied meanings, and that is why they moved readers. Poets during the Song Dynasty, however, tended to use poetry to comment on public affairs or make arguments. If that was what they wanted to achieve, why didn't they write essays instead of poems? (Tu Long: On Essay Writing)

xūyī'érjìng 虚壹而静

Open-mindedness, Concentration, and Tranquility

荀子（前313？—前238）所提出的一种用以把握日用伦常之道的心灵状态。荀子认为，需要通过心的作用才能知"道"。但人心时常处于被遮蔽的状态，只有进入"虚壹而静"的状态才能发挥应有的作用。"虚"是不使已收藏在心中的知识妨碍将要接受的东西。"壹"是使同时兼得的知识类目分明，彼此无碍。"静"是不以虚妄而混乱的知识妨碍正常的心灵活动。

This refers to a state of mind Xunzi (313?-238 BC) proposed as a way to master the Dao of general morality. He believed that one gets to know Dao through the action of one's heart and mind. But since the human heart and mind are often closed, they can only function normally when one is open-minded, concentrated, and consequently tranquil. *Xu* (虚), or open-mindedness, prevents prior knowledge from hindering the acquisition of new knowledge. *Yi* (壹), or concentration, allows one to assimilate knowledge of different categories while keeping them from interfering with each other. *Jing* (静), or tranquillity, is to keep the false and confusing knowledge from obstructing one's normal process of contemplation.

引例 Citation：

◎人何以知道？曰：心。心何以知？曰：虚壹而静。(《荀子·解蔽》)
（人如何能够知晓道？回答：用心。心如何能够知晓？回答：做到"虚壹而静"。）

How can people learn to know Dao? The answer is to use one's heart and mind. How can the heart and mind know? The answer is to achieve open-mindedness, concentration, and tranquillity. (*Xunzi*)

xué 学

Learn

　　学习，儒家认为它是成就道德生命的一种修养和教化方式。一般意义上的"学"主要指对知识的理解和掌握，而儒家所言之"学"则更多指向道德品性的养成。个人通过后天对经典和礼法的学习以及对圣贤的效法，不断培养、完善自身的德性，以成就理想的人格。道家则反对"学"，如老子主张"绝学无忧"，认为"学"会带来内心不必要的忧虑，乃至破坏人的自然状态。

To Confucianism, learning is the way to cultivate oneself to achieve moral integrity. The usual meaning of the term is to acquire knowledge and understanding, but for Confucianism it focuses more on the cultivation of moral and ethical qualities to achieve personal growth. Through learning classics and rites, and following the practices of sages, a person is able to cultivate and improve his moral standards and thus become a person of ideal qualities. Daoists, on the other hand, are against learning, and Laozi said that "fine-sounding arguments" only cause unnecessary worries, and can disrupt a person's natural state of mind.

引例 Citations：

◎学而时习之，不亦说（yuè）乎?（《论语·学而》）
（学习并按一定的时间熟习所学的内容，不也是愉快的吗？）

Isn't it a pleasure to learn and apply from time to time what one has learned? (*The Analects*)

◎君子博学而日参（cān）省乎己，则知明而行无过矣。(《荀子·劝学》)
（君子广泛学习并且每天坚持自我参验、反省，就可以做到智慧明达而行为不会有错了。）

Men of virtue, who study extensively and reflect on themselves every day, become wise and intelligent and are free from making mistakes. (*Xunzi*)

yǎngmín 养民

Nurture the People

养育人民，包括满足人民的生活需要和对人民进行教育。《尚书·大禹谟》将其作为"善政"（良好政治）的目的；为了实现这一目的，治国者必须治理、协调好"六府三事"。"六府"是指金、木、水、火、土、谷，即人民生活所需的各种物质资料；"三事"是指"正德"（端正人民品德）、"利用"（使物质资料为百姓所用）、"厚生"（使人民生活充裕）。这是一种以民为本、物质文明和精神文明兼顾并举的治国理念。

This term means to provide the people with necessities of life and educate them. According to *The Book of History*, this is what constitutes good governance. To reach this goal, the ruler must manage well the "six necessities and three matters," the six necessities being metal, wood, water, fire, land, and grain, and the three matters being fostering virtue, proper use of resources, and ensuring people's livelihood. This concept of governance, which focuses on promoting both economic and ethical progress, is people-centered.

引例 Citations：

◎德惟善政，政在养民。水、火、金、木、土、谷，惟修；正德、利用、厚生，惟和。九功惟叙；九叙惟歌。(《尚书·大禹谟》)

（帝王的德行要体现为良好的施政，施政要以养育民众为目的。水、火、金、木、土、谷六种生活资料一定要准备充足；端正德行，物尽其用，使民众富裕，这三项工作要兼顾协调。这九个方面的事情都要安排有序，九件事做好了，就会得到歌颂了。）

The king's virtue is reflected in good governance, which means to nurture the people. The people's need for water, fire, metal, wood, land, and grain must be well satisfied; and fostering virtue, proper use of resources, and ensuring people's well-being should be pursued in a coordinated way. When these nine things are accomplished in an orderly way, the king will win people's respect. (*The Book of History*)

◎夫贫生于富，弱生于强，乱生于治，危生于安。是故明王之养民也，忧之劳之，教之诲之，慎微防萌，以断其邪。（王符《潜夫论·浮侈》）

（贫困由富足中产生，衰弱由强盛中产生，动乱由太平中产生，危险由平安中产生。所以贤明的君主养育人民，经常担忧他们的疾苦，慰劳他们的艰辛，加强对他们的教诲，小心谨慎地防患于未然，断绝一切邪恶产生的源头。）

Poverty stems from wealth, weakness from strength, turmoil from stability, and danger from security. Therefore, as he nurtures the people, a wise ruler cares about their sufferings, thanks them for their work, and teaches and instructs them so as to eradicate the seeds of evil no matter how tiny they might be. (Wang Fu: *Views of a Hermit*)

yìshù 艺术

Art

原指儒家六艺及各种方术，后引申指艺术创作与审美活动。儒家的"六艺"指礼、乐、射、御、书、数等六种用以培养君子人格的教育内容，包括后世意义上的艺术；有时也指《诗》《书》《礼》《乐》《易》《春秋》六部经书。庄子（前369？—前286）则强调技与艺相通，是一种体悟道的融身心为一体的创作活动。儒家、道家与佛教关于艺术的思想，是中国艺术的内在精神与方法。中国艺术追求艺术与人生的统一、感知与体验的结合、技艺与人格的融会等，以意境为旨归。近代西方艺术学传入中国后，艺术成为人类主观精神与物态化作品相结合的技艺与创作，成为专门的学科，涵盖各类艺术。现在的艺术概念是传统艺术内涵与现代西方艺术学的有机融合。

Originally, the term referred to six forms of classical arts and various crafts, but it later extended to include artistic creation and aesthetic appreciation. The six forms of arts as defined by Confucianism are rituals, music, archery, charioteering, writing and mathematics. These constituted the basic requirements for cultivating a man of virtue. These six arts also included what later generations deemed as arts. Sometimes, the term also meant the six classics, namely, *The Book of Songs, The Book of History, The Book of Rites, The Book of Music, The Book of Changes,* and *The Spring and Autumn Annals*. Zhuangzi (369?-286 BC), on his part, emphasized the connection between crafts and arts, regarding them as physical and mental creative activities that help one gain insight into Dao. The various ideas about arts put forward by Confucian, Daoist, and Buddhist scholars defined the nature and method of Chinese arts, which seek unity between artwork and real life, fusion of senses and experiences, and integration of techniques and personality, with achieving artistic conception as the ultimate aim. Since the introduction of Western art theories in modern China, arts have become an independent discipline covering all types of arts created with skill and innovation. The concept of arts today incorporate both traditional Chinese and contemporary Western notions of arts.

引例 Citations：

◎子曰："志于道，据于德，依于仁，游于艺。"(《论语·述而》)

（孔子说："有志于行道，执守于美德，依从于仁义，游学于礼、乐、射、御、书、数六艺之间。"）

Confucius said, "One should follow Dao, adhere to virtues, embrace benevolence, and pursue freely the six arts of rituals, music, archery, charioteering, writing, and mathematics." (*The Analects*)

◎ "蓺（yì）"谓书、数、射、御，"术"谓医、方、卜、筮。(《后汉书·伏湛传》李贤注)

（"艺"指的是六书、算术、射击、驾驶车马等基本技能，"术"指的是医术、方技、卜卦、占筮等专门之学。）

Arts refer to such basic skills as writing, mathematics, archery, and charioteering. Crafts refer to such professions as medicine, fortune-telling, divination, and necromancy. (*The History of the Later Han Dynasty*)

◎艺术之兴，由来尚矣。先王以是决犹豫，定吉凶，审存亡，省祸福。(《晋书·艺术传序》)

（方术的兴起，有着久远的历史。古时的帝王通过方术来决断犹疑，判定吉凶，审度存亡，省察祸福。）

Fortune-telling has a long history. In ancient times, kings used fortune-telling to make decisions, weigh consequences, foresee fate, and judge outcomes. (*The History of the Jin Dynasty*)

yìjìng 意境

Aesthetic Conception

指文艺作品所描绘的景象与所表现的思想情感高度融合而形成的审美境界。"境"本指疆界、边界，汉末魏晋时期佛教传入中国，认为现实世界皆为空幻，唯有心灵感知才是真实的存在，"境"被认为是人的心灵感知所能达到的界域。作为文艺术语，"境"有多重含义。"意境"由唐代著名诗人王昌龄（？—756？）提出，侧重指文艺作品中主观感知到的物象与精神蕴涵相统一所达到的审美高度，其特点是"取意造境""思与境偕"。相对于"意象"，"意境"更突出文艺作品的精神蕴涵与美感的高级形态，它拓展了作品情与景、虚与实、心与物等概念的应用，提升了文艺作品及审美活动的层次。后经过历代丰富发展，"意境"成为评价文艺作品水准的重要概念，是历代经典作品层累的结果，也是优秀文艺作品必须具备的重要特征。"意境"这一术语也是外来思想文化与中华本土思想融合的典范。

The term refers to a state where the scene described in a literary or artistic work reflects the sense and sensibility intended. *Jing* (境) originally meant perimeter or boundary. With the introduction of Buddhism into China during the late Han, Wei and Jin dynasties, the idea gained popularity that the physical world was but an illusion, and that only the mind was real in existence. So *jing* came to be seen as a realm that could be attained by having sensibilities of the mind. As a literary and artistic term, *jing* has several meanings. The term *yijing* (意境) was originally put forward by renowned Tang poet Wang Changling (?-756?). It describes an intense aesthetic experience in which one's perception of an object reaches a realm of perfect union with the implication denoted by the object. Aesthetic appreciation in the mind is characterized by "projecting meaning into a scene" and "blending sentiment with scenery." In contrast with the term *yixiang* (意象 image), *yijing* (意境) fully reveals the implication and the heightened aesthetic sense that an artistic work is intended to deliver. The concept is extended to include other notions such as sentiment and scene, actual and implied meanings, or mind and object. It also raises literary and artistic works to a new realm of aesthetic appreciation. After evolving through several dynasties, this concept developed into an important criterion to judge the quality of a literary or artistic work, representing an accomplishment drawing on classical writings through ages. It has also become a hallmark for all outstanding literary and artistic works. The term also represents a perfect union between foreign thoughts and culture and those typically Chinese.

引例 Citations：

◎诗有三境：一曰物境，二曰情境，三曰意境。物境一：欲为山水诗，则张泉石云峰之境，极丽绝秀者，神之于心，处身于境，视境于心，莹然掌中，然后用思，了然境象，故得形似。情境二：娱乐愁怨，皆张于意而处于身，然后驰思，深得其情。意境三：亦张之于意而思之于心，则得其真矣。（王昌龄《诗格·诗有三境》）

（诗歌有三种境：一是物境，二是情境，三是意境。第一，物境：想作山水诗，就要尽所能扩大你对泉石、高耸入云的山峰的观察，将其中极秀丽的景色及神韵印之于心，置身其间，再于内心审视所得到的物境，直至如同在手掌上观察一样真切，然后进行构思，对所要描绘的具体物象了然于心，所以能得形似。第二，情境：欢乐、悲愁、哀怨等情绪，都要尽量扩大你对它们的认识，切身感受，然后构思，就能将这些情感深刻地表现出来。第三，意境：也同样需要扩大你对它的认识，在内心反复思索，然后就能得到意境的本真。）

A poem accomplishes aesthetic conception in three ways. The first is through objects, the second is through sentiments, and the third is through an imagined scene. 1) Through objects: If you want to write poems about landscape, you need to observe intensely springs and creeks, rocks and towering peaks, imprint their extraordinary beauty and charm on your memory, put yourself in the scene created in your mind, and view in your mind's eye the image you obtain until you can see it as vividly as if it were right on your palm. By then, you can start to think about writing the poem. A deep appreciation of the scene and its objects is instrumental in achieving a true poetic image. 2) Through sentiments: Sentiments such as happiness, pleasure, sorrow, and anger should be allowed to develop in your mind. You should experience them personally to fully grasp the nature of these emotions. This will enable you to express them in a profound way. 3) Through an imagined scene: This requires you to reach aesthetic appreciation by reflecting it in your mind time and again. Then you can capture the genuine nature of an idea. (Wang Changling: *Rules of Poetry*)

◎作诗之妙，全在意境融彻，出音声之外，乃得真味。（朱承爵《存余堂诗话》）

（作诗的妙处，全在于意境的浑融相通，超出声音之上，才能品味诗歌的本真韵味。）

A beautifully composed poem is one in which the blending of image and concept is such that it transcends that of sound and music. Only then can one savor the real charm of poetry. (Zhu Chengjue: *Comments on the Collection of Poems from Cunyutang Study*)

◎盖诗之格调有尽，吾人之意境日出而不穷。（周炳曾《〈道援堂诗集〉序》）

（大概是诗的体制、声律是有限的，而我们这些诗人的意境却每天有新创，无穷无尽。）

Poems might have limited verse forms and rhythmic patterns, but we poets are capable of creating fresh ideas every day, all the time. (Zhou Bingzeng: Preface to *Collection of Poems from Daoyuantang Study*)

yìxìng 意兴

Inspirational Appreciation

"兴"中所蕴含的意或者"兴"发时心物交会所产生的意（意义、趣味等）。是作者通过对景物感受到某种意趣、意味等之后直接创作出富有一定含义的艺术形象。这一术语主张作者将思想情感自然而然地融入对于描写对象的感受之中，并通过艺术形象和审美情趣传达出来，从而激发读者的联想，产生更丰富的领悟。

The term refers to the meaning implicit in an inspiration, or meaning and charm generated when poetic emotion encounters an external object or scene. It is an artistic image an author creates when appreciating the beauty and charm intrinsic in an object or scene. According to this term, an author should incorporate his sentiments and thoughts into the object or scene depicted to convey them through artistic images and aesthetic appreciation. This will spark the reader's imagination and thus enable him to gain a deeper appreciation of a poem.

引例 Citations：

◎凡诗，物色兼意下为好。若有物色，无意兴，虽巧亦无处用之。（王昌龄《诗格·论文意》）

（但凡诗歌，景物描写、意义与趣味兼备最好。如果只注重景物描写，缺少意兴，描写技巧再高超也用处不大。）

A good poem instills meaning and inspiration in its description of scenery and imagery. If a poem only describes scenery and fails to inspire people, no matter how eloquent the description may be, it will have little appeal. (Wang Changling: *Rules of Poetry*)

◎南朝人尚词而病于理，本朝人尚理而病于意兴，唐人尚意兴而理在其中，汉魏之诗，词、理、意兴无迹可求。（严羽《沧浪诗话·诗评》）

（南朝诗人追求辞藻而说理不足；本朝诗人崇尚说理，作品缺乏意兴；唐代诗人注重意兴同时蕴含道理；汉魏诗歌的文辞、道理和意兴自然融合在一起而不露痕迹。）

Poets of the Southern Dynasties were good at using rhetoric but weak in logic. The poets of our Song Dynasty champion logic but are weak in creating inspirational ideas. Poets of the Tang Dynasty gave equal weight to both meaning and inspiration, with logic implicit in both. The poems of the Han and Wei dynasties blended the choice of words, logic, and the inspiration imperceptibly. (Yan Yu: *Canglang's Criticism on Poetry*)

yǔzhòu 宇宙

Universe / Cosmos

本义指屋檐和栋梁，引申指空间和时间，及由无限空间和无限时间所构成的世界整体。"宇"指天地四方，也即是包括上、下、东、西、南、北的整个空间；"宙"指往古来今，也即是包括过去和未来的整个时间。"宇宙"在空间上可以无限扩展，在时间上可以无限延续。中国哲学以"宇宙论"指称探讨世界本体及世界发生发展进程的学问。

The original meaning of the term is the eave and beam of a house, while its extended meaning is time and space as well as the whole world composed of limitless time and space. The first character *yu* (宇) means heaven and earth as well as all the directions of north, south, east, west, the above, and the below. The second character *zhou* （宙）means all of time, the past, present, and future. Together, the term means infinite space and endless time. In Chinese philosophy, "theories of the universe" are concerned with the existence of the world in an ontological sense, and with its process of evolution.

引例 Citations：

◎往古来今谓之宙，四方上下谓之宇。(《淮南子·齐俗训》)
(由过去到未来的时间称为"宙"，东南西北上下的空间称为"宇"。)

The past, present, and future are called *zhou*; north, south, east, west, the above, and the below are called *yu*. (*Huainanzi*)

◎宇之表无极，宙之端无穷。(张衡《灵宪》)
("宇"的外延是没有极限的，"宙"的终始是没有穷尽的。)

Yu means space without limit; *zhou* represents time without end. (Zhang Heng: *Law of the Universe*)

yuán 元

Yuan (Origin)

事物发生的端始。"元"在天地万物之先，包括人在内的天地万物都始于"元"。"元"有多种具体的表现形式。汉代的人将"元"理解为"元气"，也即是产生和构成万物的某种原始物质材料。《周易·彖上》以"乾元""坤元"作为万物生成的端始。《春秋》纪年以"元年"为"第一年"。"元年"标志着一个新的历史时期的开始，是万物终始交替的法则在人事上的一种体现。

The term means the primal source from which all things originate, both animate and inanimate, including human beings. *Yuan* (元) manifests itself in different forms. In the Han Dynasty, it was considered a kind of primal physical material that both produced and made up the myriad things of the world. *The Book of Changes* divides *yuan* into two primal sources: the heavenly source which gives birth to the sun, moon, and stars, and the earthly source which creates all other things on earth. In *The Spring and Autumn Annals*, the term refers to the first year in its chronologies, symbolizing the start of a new historical period, and serving as the manifestation in the human world of the natural process in which things begin, end, and are replaced.

引例 Citations：

◎元者气也，无形以起，有形以分，造起天地，天地之始也。(《公羊传·隐公元年》何休注)

(元是一种气，发生时没有形状，进而分化成有形的事物，创造了天地，是天地变化的端始。)

Yuan is a vital force, without shape in the beginning. It then takes on form to create both heaven and earth, and is the source of all their transformations. (He Xiu: *Annotations on Gongyang's Commentary on The Spring and Autumn Annals*)

◎大哉乾元，万物资始，乃统天。(《周易·彖上》)

（伟大的乾元，万物依赖它开始产生，乾元统帅天的运行与效用。）

Great is the *qian* hexagram! All things owe their existence to it, and it guides the movement of heaven and creates its impact. (*The Book of Changes*)

◎《春秋》何贵乎元而言之？元者，始也。（董仲舒《春秋繁露·王道》）

(《春秋》为何以"元"为贵而言说它？因为"元"是万物之始。)

Why does *The Spring and Autumn Annals* give such importance to *yuan*? This is because *yuan* is the primordial source of all things. (Dong Zhongshu: *Luxuriant Gems of The Spring and Autumn Annals*)

zhèngzhì 政治

Decree and Governance / Politics

主要有两种用法：其一，指治理国家所施行的一切措施。"政"指统治者规定的法令、制度、秩序；"治"指对百姓的管理、治理，是"政"的具体实施。其二，指国家治理达到稳定良好的状态，即政治清明、经济繁荣、天下太平。近代以降，"政治"转指政府、政党、社会团体或个人在国内、国际事务中采取的政策、措施和行为等。

The term has two meanings. First, it refers to all measures for governing a country. *Zheng* (政) stands for decrees, rules, and ordinances, and *zhi* (治) refers to their implementation, that is, the way in which the people are governed. Second, it refers to a state of stable and sound governance of the country, with an efficient and clean government, a prosperous economy, and a peaceful society. In modern times, the term is used in the sense of "politics," as it refers to policies, measures, and actions that governments, political parties, social groups, or individuals adopt in domestic or international affairs.

引例 Citations：

◎道洽政治，泽润生民。(《尚书·毕命》)

(教化普施，政治清明，恩泽惠及百姓。)

Shaping people's mind through popularizing education and exercising good governance will benefit the people. (*The Book of History*)

◎政以治民，刑以正邪。(《左传·隐公十一年》)

(以政令治理百姓，以刑法匡正邪恶。)

Decrees are adopted to maintain public order, while punishments are meted out to eliminate evil. (*Zuo's Commentary on The Spring and Autumn Annals*)

zhīxíng 知行

Knowledge and Application

"知"指对人伦日用之道的认知和体察，"行"指践行人伦日用之道。中国古代所讨论的"知行"，并不是一般意义上的对外物的认知以及利用和改造外物的行为，而是针对人伦日用之道的体认与践行。人通过目见耳闻或心思感悟等不同方式实现"知"。对于"知""行"的难易，或认为知难行易，或认为知易行难，或认为知难行亦难。而在"知""行"关系上，有人主张知行合一，也有人认为知行有别。这些对"知行"的理解决定了不同的道德养成及人伦教化方式。

"Knowledge" refers to awareness and examination of the principles underlying

143

human relations in everyday life, and "application" refers to the implementation of these principles in everyday life. "Knowledge and application," used in ancient China, were not in the general sense of having knowledge of external objects, or taking action to utilize and transform external things. Rather, they were recognition and application of principles underlying human relations in everyday life. One acquires "knowledge" in different ways: through visual perception, hearing, or mental reflection and insight. Some people think that "knowledge" is difficult and that "application" is easy. Some think that "knowledge" is easy and that "application" is difficult. Some think that "knowledge" and "application" are equally difficult. As for the relationship between "knowledge" and "application", some maintain that knowledge and application are united as one. Others think that knowledge and application are separate. These varied understanding of "knowledge and application" determine different ways of fostering virtue and of instruction concerning human relations.

引例 Citations：

◎非知之实难，将在行之。(《左传·昭公十年》)
（并不是难在"知"，而是难在"行"。）

To know is not the hard part; to apply is. (*Zuo's Commentary on The Spring and Autumn Annals*)

◎不闻不若闻之，闻之不若见之，见之不若知之，知之不若行之，学至于行之而止矣。(《荀子·儒效》)
（不听闻不如听闻，听闻不如亲眼见到，见到不如体认，体认不如践行，学问至于践行就达到极致了。）

Not having heard something is not as good as having heard it; having heard it is not as good as having seen it; having seen it is not as good as knowing it; knowing it is not as good as putting it into practice. Learning reaches the ultimate stage when it is being applied. (*Xunzi*)

zhǐgēwéiwǔ 止戈为武

Stopping War Is a True Craft of War.

  能制止战争、平息战乱才是真正的武功。这是春秋时代楚庄王（？—前591）根据"武"字的字形提出的著名的军事思想。"止"即止息；"戈"即武器，借指战争。将"武"释为止战，既符合以形表意的汉字文化特质，也表现了中国人以武禁暴的军事政治观及崇尚和平、反对战争的文明精神。

To be able to stop war is a true craft of war. This famous military view was first raised by King Zhuang of Chu (?-591 BC) in the Spring and Autumn Period, on the basis of the structure of the Chinese character *wu* (武). *Wu* is composed of *zhi* (止), which means to stop; and *ge* (戈), which means dagger-axe or weapons and is used here in the metaphorical sense of warfare. To interpret *wu* as stopping war was consistent with the cultural characteristics of Chinese characters. It also expresses the Chinese people's thinking of using military means to stop violence and their love of peace and opposition to war.

引例 Citation：

◎仓颉作书，"止""戈"为"武"。圣人以武禁暴整乱，止息干戈，非以为残而兴纵之也。(《汉书·武五子传赞》)

（仓颉造字，由"止""戈"合成一个"武"字。圣人使用武力禁止残暴，平定动乱，止息战争，而不是为了残杀、毁灭[对方]而滥用武力。）

When Cang Jie created Chinese script, he put *zhi* (止 stop) and *ge* (戈 dagger-axe) together to make *wu* (武 war). To stop war, sages used military force to quell violence and turmoil. They did not abuse their military power to commit atrocities of killing and destroying their opponents. (*The History of the Han Dynasty*)

zìqiáng-bùxī 自强不息

Strive Continuously to Strengthen Oneself

自己努力向上，强大自己，永不懈怠停息。古人认为，天体出于自身的本性而运行，刚健有力，周而复始，一往无前永不停息。君子取法于"天"，也应发挥自己的能动性、主动性，勤勉不懈，奋发进取。这是中国人参照天体运行状态树立的执政理念和自身理想。它和"厚德载物"一起构成了中华民族精神的基本品格。

The term means that one should strive continuously to strengthen himself. Ancient Chinese believed that heavenly bodies move in accordance with their own nature in a vigorous and forever forward-going cycle. A man of virtue, who follows the law of heaven, should be fully motivated and work diligently to strengthen himself. This is the Chinese view on governance and self development, established with reference to the movement of heavenly bodies. Together with the notion that a true gentleman has ample virtue and carries all things, it constitutes the fundamental trait of the Chinese nation.

引例 Citations：

◎天行健，君子以自强不息。(《周易·象上》)

（天的运行刚健有力，一往无前，君子应像天一样，奋发图强，永不停息。）

Just as heaven keeps moving forward vigorously, a man of virtue should strive continuously to strengthen himself. (*The Book of Changes*)

◎自人君公卿至于庶人，不自强而功成者，天下未之有也。(《淮南子·修务训》)

（自帝王公卿到普通百姓，不奋发进取就能建立功业的，普天之下没有这样的事情。）

Neither monarchs, ministers, nor commoners have ever achieved great accomplishments in the world without first striving to strengthen themselves. (*Huainanzi*)

◎外有敌国，则其计先自强。自强者，人畏我，我不畏人。(《宋史·董槐传》)

（外有敌对的国家，那我们首先要谋求使自己强大。如果自己强大了，敌国就会畏惧我们，我们就不会畏惧他们。）

Facing hostile countries, we must first of all strive to become strong. If we have strengthened ourselves, enemy states will fear us and we will not fear them. (*The History of the Song Dynasty*)

zǒngjí 总集

General Collection / Anthology

汇集多人诗文作品的集子（与汇集某一作家诗文作品的"别集"相对）。总集的体例，从内容角度看，有"全集式"总集与"选集式"总集；按照收录时代范围，可分为通代总集和断代总集；按所收录作品的文体，可分为专辑同一文体的总集和汇集各种文体作品的总集。总集中最有代表性的为南朝梁昭明太子萧统（501—531）及文士共同编选的《文选》。《文选》选录先秦至梁初各类文体 700 余篇文学作品，以内容与文采并茂为收录标准，不收经、史、子类文章（仅收史传中的少量序、论、赞），反映出当时人们的文学观念，对于后世文学发展影响深远。

Zongji (总集) is a collection of various authors' poems and proses (distinct from *bieji* [别集], a collection of a particular author's literary works). In terms of content, an anthology could be either comprehensive or limited in selection. Chronically, an anthology can be a general collection spanning written history, or a general collection from one dynasty. In terms of the genre of collected works, it can be divided into collections of a specific genre and collections of various genres. The most representative anthology is *Selections of Refined Literature* compiled and edited jointly by Xiao Tong (501-531, Crown Prince Zhaoming of the Liang Dynasty during the Southern Dynasties) and his literary advisors. *Selections of Refined Literature* consists of more than 700 outstanding literary pieces of various genres from pre-Qin through the early Liang. It does not include any work that belongs to the categories of *jing* (经 Confucian classics), *shi* (史 history), or *zi* (子 thoughts of ancient scholars and schools), but does include a small number of prefaces, commentaries, and eulogies from *shi*. *Selections of Refined Literature* reflects the literary trend of the time and exerted a far-reaching impact on the development of Chinese literature in the years to come.

引例 Citations：

◎总集者，以建安之后，辞赋转繁，众家之集，日以滋广，晋代挚虞……合

而编之，谓为《流别》。(《隋书·经籍志》)

(总集之由来，是因为汉建安之后，辞赋创作数量繁多，各家的文集，日益增广。于是晋朝的挚虞……把它们合编在一起，称之为《流别》。)

An anthology was compiled because a large number of works of *ci* (辞) and *fu* (赋) were created, and different collections of various authors were widespread. They were put together under the title of *Literary Trends and Schools* by Zhi Yu of the Jin Dynasty. (*The History of the Sui Dynasty*)

◎总集盖源于《尚书》、《诗》三百篇，洎(jì)王逸《楚词》、挚虞《流别》后，日兴纷出，其义例可得而言。(马其昶《〈桐城古文集略〉序》)

(总集大体源于《尚书》《诗经》，及至王逸编选《楚辞》、挚虞编选《流别》之后，纷纷面世，它的主旨和体例才可以论说清楚。)

The form of anthology originated from *The Book of History* and *The Book of Songs*. After *Annotations on the Odes of Chu* and *Literary Trends and Schools* were compiled and edited by Wang Yi and Zhi Yu respectively, various anthologies began to appear, and became clear in themes and formats. (Ma Qichang: Preface to *Selected Classic Works of the Tongcheng School*)

术语表 List of Concepts

英文	中文
Add Pupils to the Eyes of a Painted Dragon / Render the Final Touch	画龙点睛
Aesthetic Conception Transcends Concrete Objects Described.	境生象外
Aesthetic Conception	意境
All People Are My Brothers and Sisters, and All Things Are My Companions.	民胞物与
Art	艺术
Attached to the Land and Unwilling to Move	安土重迁
Be Cultured and Refined	斯文
Be on Alert Against Potential Danger When Living in Peace	居安思危
Beat Swords into Plowshares / Turn War into Peace	化干戈为玉帛
Bense (Original Character)	本色
Capital / Metropolis	都
Capital of a Country	京（京师）
Carefree	逍遥
Changing the Mandate / Revolution	革命
Chaos	浑沌
Chuci (Ode of Chu)	楚辞
Dao of Painting	画道
Dao Operates Naturally.	道法自然

英文	中文
Decree and Governance / Politics	政治
Denouncing Unjust Wars	非攻
Distinct Subject and Artistic Taste	别材别趣
Distinction Between Man and Heaven	天人之分
Eight Trigrams	八卦
Elegant Subtlety	神韵
Expressiveness	辞达
Family-state / Country	国家
Fighting a War with a Moral Justification	师出有名
Five Classics	五经
Fortress / City	城
Four Books	四书
Four Initiators	四端
Four Seas	四海
General Collection / Anthology	总集
Going Too Far Is as Bad as Falling Short.	过犹不及
Govern and Help the People / Economy	经济
Great Virtue Is Like Water.	上善若水
Guoti	国体
Harmony but Not Uniformity	和而不同
Have Ample Virtue and Carry All Things	厚德载物
Heart-to-heart Communication	会心

英文	中文
Heaven and Man Are United as One.	天人合一
Historical Poetry	诗史
Individual Collection	别集
Inspirational Appreciation	意兴
Interaction Between the Mind and the Subject Matter	神与物游
Jingjie (Visionary World)	境界
Junzi (Man of Virtue)	君子
Knowledge and Application	知行
Kun (The Earth Symbol)	坤
Learn	学
Li (Rites / Social Norms / Propriety)	礼
Literary Flexibility	活法
Literary Writing	文章
Literature / Scholars / Education Officials	文学
Lord / Nobility / Monarch	君
Magically Natural, Overly Crafted	化工 / 画工
Mandate / Destiny	命
Mild, Gentle, Sincere, and Broad-minded	温柔敦厚
Name and Substance	名实
Nurture the People	养民
Once the Lips Are Gone, the Teeth Will Feel Cold.	唇亡齿寒
Open-mindedness, Concentration, and Tranquility	虚壹而静

英文	中文
Outside the Four Seas / Overseas	海外
Painting in Poetry, Poetry in Painting	诗中有画，画中有诗
People of Wu and Yue Are in the Same Boat.	吴越同舟
Petty Man	小人
Prevailing Features	气象
Qian	乾
Qujing (Conceptualize an Aesthetic Feeling)	取境
Reflecting / Thinking	思
Renwen (Human Culture)	人文
Seek Truth from Facts	实事求是
Self-driven Development	独化
Shield and Fortress / Dukes and Princes	干城
Sitting with Clothes Unbuttoned and Legs Stretching Out	解衣盘礴
Son of Heaven	天子
Stopping War Is a True Craft of War.	止戈为武
Strive Continuously to Strengthen Oneself	自强不息
Study of Ancient Classics Should Meet Present Needs.	经世致用
Study Things to Acquire Knowledge	格物致知
Style Differentiation	辨体
Subtle Insight	妙悟
Supreme Ruler / Ruler of Heaven	上帝

英文	中文
The Law Does Not Favor the Rich and Powerful.	法不阿贵
Three Metaphysical Classics	三玄
Ti	体
Toughness and Softness	刚柔
Trigrams / Hexagrams and Component Lines	卦爻
Understand Things and Succeed in One's Endeavors	开物成务
Universal Love	兼爱
Universe / Cosmos	宇宙
Virtue Comparison	比德
Way of Man	人道
What Is Above Form / The Metaphysical	形而上
What Is Under Form / The Physical	形而下
Within the Four Seas / Within the Country	海内
Writing and Writing Technique	文笔
Xingji (Association and Inner Sustenance)	兴寄
Xingqu (Charm)	兴趣
Yuan (Origin)	元

中国历史年代简表 A Brief Chronology of Chinese History

夏 Xia Dynasty		2070-1600 BC
商 Shang Dynasty		1600-1046 BC
周 Zhou Dynasty		1046-256 BC
周 Zhou Dynasty	西周 Western Zhou Dynasty	1046-771 BC
	东周 Eastern Zhou Dynasty	770-256 BC
秦 Qin Dynasty		221-206 BC
汉 Han Dynasty		206 BC-AD 220
汉 Han Dynasty	西汉 Western Han Dynasty	206 BC-AD 25
	东汉 Eastern Han Dynasty	25-220
三国 Three Kingdoms		220-280
三国 Three Kingdoms	魏 Kingdom of Wei	220-265
	蜀 Kingdom of Shu	221-263
	吴 Kingdom of Wu	222-280
晋 Jin Dynasty		265-420
晋 Jin Dynasty	西晋 Western Jin Dynasty	265-317
	东晋 Eastern Jin Dynasty	317-420
南北朝 Southern and Northern Dynasties		420-589
南北朝 Southern and Northern Dynasties	南朝 Southern Dynasties	420-589
	南朝 Southern Dynasties — 宋 Song Dynasty	420-479
	齐 Qi Dynasty	479-502
	梁 Liang Dynasty	502-557
	陈 Chen Dynasty	557-589

南北朝 Southern and Northern Dynasties	北朝 Northern Dynasties		386-581
	北朝 Northern Dynasties	北魏 Northern Wei Dynasty	386-534
		东魏 Eastern Wei Dynasty	534-550
		北齐 Northern Qi Dynasty	550-577
		西魏 Western Wei Dynasty	535-556
		北周 Northern Zhou Dynasty	557-581
隋 Sui Dynasty			581-618
唐 Tang Dynasty			618-907
五代 Five Dynasties			907-960
五代 Five Dynasties	后梁 Later Liang Dynasty		907-923
	后唐 Later Tang Dynasty		923-936
	后晋 Later Jin Dynasty		936-947
	后汉 Later Han Dynasty		947-950
	后周 Later Zhou Dynasty		951-960
宋 Song Dynasty			960-1279
宋 Song Dynasty	北宋 Northern Song Dynasty		960-1127
	南宋 Southern Song Dynasty		1127-1279
辽 Liao Dynasty			907-1125
西夏 Western Xia Dynasty			1038-1227
金 Jin Dynasty			1115-1234
元 Yuan Dynasty			1206-1368
明 Ming Dynasty			1368-1644
清 Qing Dynasty			1616-1911
中华民国 Republic of China			1912-1949
中华人民共和国 People's Republic of China			Founded on October 1, 1949